"This book is essential reading for those educators seeking to transform the learning experiences of their students. It provides an inspiring view of learning that is centered on the student and connected to the outdoor environment and issues of social justice."

Julie A. Luft, *distinguished research professor and NSTA and AAAS fellow, University of Georgia College of Education*

"Passionate science educators don't enter their profession in pursuit of standardized tests or chapter review questions. We want to pass on the same impactful experiences of challenge and discovery that inspired us. But somewhere between the idealism of preparing to teach and the reality of—well, real life, we may make some compromises. This book bridges the gap between what is possible and what is probable when it comes to teaching inquiry-based science. They show students that scientific inquiry is not locked in ivory towers but is based on observations and testable questions about the world around us. They show teachers that school grounds, simple materials, and creativity are fertile grounds for growing scientific literacy. Let these lessons allow you to compromise on the extra time you sacrifice to develop inquiry-based lessons without compromising on engaging students in a holistic way that leaves a lasting impact."

Caroline Pechuzal, *biology teacher, Canyon Del Oro High School*

"Justice-first science teaching involves practices that few educators were trained for, but Dr. Blonder and colleagues make this goal accessible by providing frameworks, tools, and best of all, real-life examples of equitable learning by children at different grade levels. Each chapter lays out cases of teachers empowering students through authentic place-based experiences, choice, and strategic forms of support as youth investigate complex phenomena that matter to them in the real world."

Mark Windschitl, *professor of science education, University of Washington, and author of* Ambitious Science Teaching

"Scientists study and interpret nature in and by means of real places. Our students should be able to do the same. This Handbook offers a wealth of ideas, tools, and examples to foster place-based, student-centered scientific learning."

Steven Semken, *professor, School of Earth and Space Exploration, and affiliate faculty, Teachers College, Arizona State University*

"What a great contribution to place-based science education literature! This book is chock full of guidance for how to structure learning outside with great examples of actual projects conducted with actual students. It also provides great examples of student worksheets, assessment rubrics, and scientific methodologies. It's a remarkably useful book."

David Sobel, *author of* Place-Based Education: Connecting Classrooms and Communities, *and professor emeritus, Antioch University New England*

"This Handbook is a practicable guide for anyone seeking to provide youth with supportive and meaningful outdoor classroom experiences. It's a grounding breath of fresh air for educators and community leaders alike."

Ruby Rodriguez, *Director of Programs & Operations, Latino Outdoors*

Place-Based Scientific Inquiry

Learn how to facilitate scientific inquiry projects by getting out of the classroom and connecting to the natural environment—in your schoolyard, or in your community!

Providing a contemporary perspective on how to do scientific inquiry in ways that can make teachers' lives easier and students' experiences better, this book draws on authentic inquiry, engaging with communities, and teaching through project-based learning to help students design and carry out scientific inquiry projects that are grounded in their local places. This accessible guide will help you to develop skills around facilitation, team building, and learning outdoors in schoolyards and parks, acting as a go-to toolkit for teachers to help build confidence and skills in these areas.

Written according to the Next Generation Science Standards, this book supports teachers in fostering community engagement and a justice-first classroom. The approachable resources included in this book will help teachers with all levels of experience succeed in empowering students grades 3–12 in their science learning.

Additional support materials, including template documents for student use and for teacher planning, as well as examples of real student work, are available online.

Benjamin Wong Blonder is an assistant professor and ecologist at the University of California at Berkeley.

Ja'Nya Banks was a special education teacher and now is a doctoral student in education policy at the University of California at Berkeley.

Austin R. Cruz is an ecologist and educator at the University of Arizona.

Anna Dornhaus is a professor at the University of Arizona studying complex systems and insect behavior.

R. Keating Godfrey is a neuroscientist at the Florida Museum of Natural History with a background in hands-on, outdoor science education and job skills training.

Joshua S. Hoskinson is an adjunct faculty member at Tohono O'odham Community College.

Rebecca Lipson taught middle school science, math, and special education for eight years and served as the assistant director of education at the University of Arizona Sky School.

Pacifica Sommers is an ecologist and educator at the University of Colorado at Boulder.

Christy Coverdale Stewart has 35 years of experience as a middle and high school science teacher, curriculum specialist, and teacher coach.

Alan Strauss has a background in disability studies and is the director of the University of Arizona's Mount Lemmon Science Center and Sky School.

Also Available from Routledge Eye On Education
www.routledge.com/k-12

Teaching Towards Green Schools
Transforming K-12 Education through Sustainable Practices
By Linda H. Plevyak

Learning in the Age of Climate Disasters
Teacher and Student Empowerment Beyond Futurephobia
By Maggie Favretti

Teaching Climate Change for Grades 6-12
Empowering Science Teachers to Take on the Climate Crisis Through NGSS
By Kelley Le

Inquiry-Based Science Activities in Grade 6-12
Meeting the NGSS
By Patrick Brown and James Concannon

Place-Based Scientific Inquiry

A Practical Handbook for Teaching Outside

Benjamin Wong Blonder,
Ja'Nya Banks, Austin Cruz,
Anna Dornhaus, R. Keating Godfrey,
Joshua S. Hoskinson,
Rebecca Lipson, Pacifica Sommers,
Christy Coverdale Stewart,
and Alan Strauss

Designed cover image: © Rebecca Lipson

First published 2023
by Routledge
605 Third Avenue, New York, NY 10158

and by Routledge
4 Park Square, Milton Park, Abingdon, Oxon, OX14 4RN

Routledge is an imprint of the Taylor & Francis Group, an informa business

© 2023 Benjamin Wong Blonder, Ja'Nya Banks, Austin Cruz, Anna Dornhaus, R. Keating Godfrey, Joshua S. Hoskinson, Rebecca Lipson, Pacifica Sommers, Christy Coverdale Stewart, and Alan Strauss

The right of Benjamin Wong Blonder, Ja'Nya Banks, Austin Cruz, Anna Dornhaus, R. Keating Godfrey, Joshua S. Hoskinson, Rebecca Lipson, Pacifica Sommers, Christy Coverdale Stewart, and Alan Strauss to be identified as authors of this work has been asserted in accordance with sections 77 and 78 of the Copyright, Designs and Patents Act 1988.

The Open Access version of this book, available at www.taylorfrancis.com, has been made available under a Creative Commons Attribution 4.0 license.

Trademark notice: Product or corporate names may be trademarks or registered trademarks, and are used only for identification and explanation without intent to infringe.

Library of Congress Cataloging-in-Publication Data
Names: Blonder, Benjamin Wong, author.
Title: Place-based scientific inquiry : a practical handbook for teaching outside / Benjamin Wong Blonder, Ja'Nya Banks, Austin R. Cruz, Anna Dornhaus,
R. Keating Godfrey, Joshua S. Hoskinson, Rebecca Lipson, Pacifica Sommers, Christy Coverdale Stewart, Alan Strauss.
Description: New York, NY : Routledge, 2023. | Includes bibliographical references.
Identifiers: LCCN 2023004790 (print) | LCCN 2023004791 (ebook) |
ISBN 9781032434162 (hardback) | ISBN 9781032434155 (paperback) |
ISBN 9781003367192 (ebook)
Subjects: LCSH: Place-based education. | Outdoor education. | Community and school.
Classification: LCC LC239 .B56 2023 (print) | LCC LC239 (ebook) |
DDC 371.3/84--dc23/eng/20230411
LC record available at https://lccn.loc.gov/2023004790
LC ebook record available at https://lccn.loc.gov/2023004791

ISBN: 978-1-032-43416-2 (hbk)
ISBN: 978-1-032-43415-5 (pbk)
ISBN: 978-1-003-36719-2 (ebk)

DOI: 10.4324/9781003367192

Typeset in Optima
by KnowledgeWorks Global Ltd.

Access the Support Material: www.routledge.com/9781032434155

Contents

About the Authors   xiii
Acknowledgments   xv

1. **Introduction**   1
   1.1 A Desert Story   1
   1.2 How to Use the Book   2

2. **Guiding Concepts**   3
   2.1 Justice-First Science Teaching   3
   2.2 Place-Based Teaching   4
   2.3 Inquiry-Based Teaching   7
   2.4 Teaching Outside   8
   2.5 Centering Student Identity   10
   2.6 Meeting the Next Generation Science Standards   12
   2.7 Learning Beyond the NGSS   14
   2.8 Decolonizing Teaching   15
   2.9 Linking to Indigenous Science   18

3. **Setting Scope and Expectations**   20
   3.1 Your Role as Teacher   20
   3.2 Choosing a Topic   24
   3.3 Scheduling and Time Considerations   26
   3.4 Scaffolding Projects into Your Curriculum   32
   3.5 Cost Considerations   35
   3.6 Place Considerations   38
   3.7 Student Identity Considerations   42
   3.8 Universal Design, Special Needs, and Disability   46

Contents

4. Acquiring Resources and Planning Safe Logistics — 53
    4.1 Partnering with Volunteers — 53
    4.2 Acquiring Equipment and Collecting Data at Low Cost — 58
    4.3 Safety and Logistical Preparation — 65

5. Getting Started via Exploration and Team Building — 73
    5.1 Dividing Students into Groups — 73
    5.2 Using Notebooks — 75
    5.3 Exploration, Observation, and Sense of Place — 79
    5.4 Acquiring Background Information — 87
    5.5 Recognizing Relationships and Responsibility to Place — 90

6. Facilitating Teams and Resolving Conflict — 97
    6.1 Small-Group Facilitation — 97
    6.2 Setting Behavioral Expectations — 102
    6.3 Encouraging Positive Behavior from Individuals — 107
    6.4 Encouraging Positive Behavior from Groups — 113
    6.5 Team Building — 118
    6.6 Team Contracts and Check-Ins — 125
    6.7 Handling Multiple Groups — 129
    6.8 Getting Groups Back on Track — 132

7. Developing a Question and Study Design — 136
    7.1 Facilitating Question Development — 136
    7.2 Building a Strong Question — 141
    7.3 Designing a Study and Using an Anchor Chart — 147
    7.4 Identifying Multiple Hypotheses and Predictions, or Not — 161

8. Planning Data Collection — 172
    8.1 Choosing How Much to Measure — 172
    8.2 Choosing What to Do (Protocols, Checklists, and Datasheets) — 176
    8.3 Choosing Roles — 179

9. Collecting Data Outside — 183
    9.1 Practicing Collecting Data — 183
    9.2 Collecting Data — 185
    9.3 Securing Data — 192

10.	**Analyzing and Sense-Making**	198
	10.1 Drawing Conclusions from Data	198
	10.2 Visually Interpreting Results	205
	10.3 Statistical Tests	212
11.	**Reflecting and Recognizing Success**	218
	11.1 Reflection	218
	11.2 Recognition	223
12.	**Sharing Outcomes**	226
	12.1 How and Why to Share Projects	226
	12.2 Supporting Presentation Development	232
	12.3 Holding a Community Event	237
13.	**Assessing Learning**	243
	13.1 Why (or Why Not) to Assess	243
	13.2 Student-Centered Reflection and Feedback	247
14.	**Conclusion**	252
	14.1 What Students and Teachers Say	252
	14.2 Overcoming Common Fears	253
	14.3 Starting Small and Dreaming Big	254

References	256
Index	263

Available to Download Online:

Appendix 1: *Example Student-Facing Documents*
   A1.1 *Anchor chart*
   A1.2 *Data entry planning table*
   A1.3 *Datasheet*
   A1.4 *Team contract – Elementary school (3–5)*
   A1.5 *Team contract – Middle and high school (6–12)*
   A1.6 *Mid-project check-in – All grade levels*

Appendix 2: *Example Teacher-Facing Documents*
   A2.1 *Risk management plan*
   A2.2 *Packing list for students/volunteers*
   A2.3 *Packing list for teachers*

Appendix 3: *Example Rubrics*
A3.1 *Project rubric – Elementary school (3–5)*
A3.2 *Project rubric – Middle and high school (6–12)*
A3.3 *Teamwork rubric – All grade levels*
A3.4 *Presentation rubric – All grade levels*
A3.5 *Student choice and independence rubric – All grade levels*

Appendix 4: *Example Schedules*
A4.1 *Elementary school (3–5)*
A4.2 *Middle school (6–8)*
A4.3 *High school (9–12)*

Appendix 5: *Example Projects*
A5.1 *Elementary school, 3rd grade: Flying Over the School*
A5.2 *Elementary school, 3rd grade: Using Plants to Dye Fabric*
A5.3 *Elementary school, 3rd grade: A Thorny Issue*
A5.4 *Elementary school, 4th grade: Shades of Green*
A5.5 *Elementary school, 5th grade: Rainy Days*
A5.6 *Middle school, 7th–8th grade: Ladybug Habitats*
A5.7 *Middle school, 7th–8th grade: Ladybug Behaviors*
A5.8 *Middle school, 8th grade: Optimal Shelters*
A5.9 *High school, mixed grade levels: Making Natural Pigments*
A5.10 *High school, mixed grade levels: Deciphering the Fetid Goosefoot*
A5.11 *High school, mixed grade levels: The Effects of Rainfall on Spring Water Chemistry*
A5.12 *High school, mixed grade levels: A Trail Left Behind*

About the Authors

Benjamin Wong Blonder, PhD, is an assistant professor and ecologist at the University of California at Berkeley. He co-developed the University of Arizona Sky School and taught middle school science via a National Science Foundation fellowship and via AmeriCorps service. He was recognized by the White House as a "Champion of Change" for environmental stewardship work.

Ja'Nya Banks, MEd, is a doctoral student focused on education policy at the University of California at Berkeley. Her master's work focused on special education and education policy. After teaching secondary school, she worked with preservice teachers on engaging with racial identity in the classroom and taught undergraduate courses on critical education.

Austin R. Cruz, MA, is an ecologist and educator at the University of Arizona. He is active in teaching and instructor training at the Sky School and has extensive pedagogical experience in formal and informal science education and environmental education, particularly with historically excluded youth in the United States and Latin America.

Anna Dornhaus, PhD, is a professor who studies complex systems and insect behavior at the University of Arizona. In teaching, she realized that students are often not taught how science works. She became active doing hands-on science with elementary school students and in teacher development.

R. Keating Godfrey, PhD, is a neuroscientist with a background in hands-on, outdoor science education and job skills training. She is interested in urban ecology and supporting access to science. She managed the Sky School's research apprenticeship program, supporting undergraduate mentorship of K–12 students in outdoor science fair projects.

About the Authors

Joshua S. Hoskinson, MS, MA, is a former Sky School instructor with a background in ecology and environmental science. He is passionate about understanding how students learn science and science's role in society. He is active in science education and outreach initiatives at the University of Arizona, Tohono O'odham Community College, and Arizona State University.

Rebecca Lipson taught science, math, and special education for eight years in Tucson's public schools. She was Sky School's assistant director for education from 2013 to 2021. Her work focuses on providing young people with experiential learning opportunities, with the goal of breaking down barriers to success in STEM disciplines for those who have been historically excluded.

Pacifica Sommers, PhD, piloted and co-developed the University of Arizona Sky School program, funded by a NASA Space Grant fellowship, after teaching in junior high classrooms as a National Science Foundation fellow. Since moving to the University of Colorado at Boulder, she has continued building inquiry-based outdoor teaching programs via Girls on Rock, a tuition-free expedition for high school girls to explore the mountains through science, art, and rock climbing.

Christy Coverdale Stewart, MEd, has 35 years of experience in education as a teacher, curriculum specialist, and teacher coach with a focus on cross-curricular, project-based/inquiry learning and a continual eye to personal application and global connection. She was a Southern Arizona Writing Fellow and completed the Systems Thinking in the Sciences program at the University of Arizona.

Alan Strauss, PhD, is the director of the University of Arizona's Mount Lemmon Science Center and Sky School, providing leadership and direction for public astronomy programs and for K–12 science programs.

Acknowledgments

Open-access publication is supported by the University of California at Berkeley's Life Science Initiative and the Berkeley Research Impact Initiative.

All author royalties from this book are being donated to the University of Arizona Foundation, in support of student access to the University of Arizona's Sky School. This program provides multiday K–12 STEM programs to public schools in Arizona. Students carry out self-directed, place-based outdoor inquiry projects in schoolyards, parks, deserts, and forests.

We respectfully acknowledge the University of Arizona Sky School is on the land and territories of Indigenous peoples. Today, Arizona is home to 22 federally recognized tribes, with Tucson being home to the O'odham and the Yaqui. Committed to diversity and inclusion, the University strives to build sustainable relationships with sovereign Native Nations and Indigenous communities through education offerings, partnerships, and community service.

Work has been supported by the Agnese Nelms Haury Program in Environment and Social Justice, Arizona State University's School of Life Sciences, Barry Boyce, BBVA Compass Bank, Dan and Carolyn Neff, the National Science Foundation, the National Aeronautics and Space Administration, the North Face's Explore Fund, the United Kingdom's Natural Environment Research Council, the University of Arizona's College of Science and Steward Observatory, Ed Beshore and Amy Phillips, and the Willingham Foundation.

We are indebted to the Tucson education community, especially Janna Acevedo, David Baker, Joan Gilbert, Anna Heyer, Jeremy Jonas, Adelle McNiece, and Gabriel Trujillo. The Coronado National Forest (United States Forest Service) has supported our use of public land. At

Acknowledgments

the University of Arizona, we have been supported by Judie Bronstein, Sanlyn Buxner, Carmala Garzione, Elliott Cheu, Buell Jannuzi, Rob McGehee, Pamela Pelletier, Barry Roth, Joaquin Ruiz, Kathleen Walker. Our work builds on programs developed by Karla Eitel, Greg Fizzell, Steve Hollenhorst, Gary Thompson, and others at the University of Idaho's McCall Outdoor Science School. Writing feedback was provided by Mandy Becker, Jaime Camero, Chelia McCoo Dogan, Karla Eitel, Joan Gilbert, Caitlin Hawley, Sunggye Hong, April Luehmann, Lauren Madden, Vicki Massey, Adelle McNiece, L. Winifred Sloan, and an anonymous reviewer. Copy editing was provided by Breanne Adkins, Becky Ford, Casey Kearney, and Amrita Rabi Sankar.

We are grateful to all the students whose photos and work are included in the book. Faces, names, and other identifying features are pixelated for privacy. Please imagine the many smiles that we are not able to show to the reader.

Introduction

1.1 A Desert Story

"Who waters the desert?" asked a seventh-grade student during science class at a public middle school in Tucson, Arizona. The city is situated in the Sonoran Desert, a landscape filled with saguaros and wildflowers, coyotes and roadrunners, and shaped for millennia by the Tohono O'Odham and Pascua Yaqui Indigenous peoples. Within a few miles of the city's outskirts are vast expanses of land. All of this might make you imagine that several answer to this question would have come to this student's mind, but none did. This student had never had the opportunity to leave the city and see the effects of the monsoon rains on the land, nor had they any connection to people who would have prioritized sharing this knowledge, nor had they had the chance to think through the question for themselves. They are not alone, and they deserve better—as do many other young people.

This book is an effort to improve teaching practices in formal science education. It is written to help classroom teachers extend their approaches to teaching in ways that connect all students to their places and to themselves—safely, confidently, and effectively. If you feel that your students deserve to develop a critical and thoughtful perspective around nature, people, and the relationship between them, this book is for you. If you want to transform your classroom from an indoor space to a schoolyard, park or neighborhood, this book is for you. If you want to do all this while also meeting the Next Generation Science Standards, this book is for you.

DOI: 10.4324/9781003367192-1
This chapter has been made available under a CC-BY license.

1.2 How to Use the Book

You do not have to read this book cover to cover. It is a set of resources to draw from while developing your teaching practice.

The book is organized into an overview of key ideas and motivations (Chapter 2), step-by-step guidance through a project lifecycle (Chapters 3–14), and a set of example documents (Appendices 1–5).

Each chapter is organized into one or more subsections. *Concepts* explores the key ideas behind the topic. *Equity and inclusion* gives guidance for ensuring these ideas serve all of your students. *Implementation* provides practical steps for putting these ideas into action. *Grade-level differentiation* helps to adapt these ideas in age-appropriate ways. *Examples* showcases actual student work. Each chapter also provides teacher-friendly references to consult for deeper engagement.

2 Guiding Concepts

2.1 Justice-First Science Teaching

Why teach science? One answer is that it helps students meet the educational standards set by the state, developing skills that are considered valuable, which in turn provides them access to future life pathways and socioeconomic progress. A second answer is that it helps the state by supporting future economic growth through scientific discovery and workforce training. A third answer is that it helps students deepen their knowledge and their reasoning about the world, individually making them better able to appreciate and understand the world around them.

A fourth answer is that teaching science helps promote justice. Science is a leverage point because it provides tools for inquiry about the natural world and also provides knowledge about the ways in which human society depends on the natural world. Justice-first science teaching requires reckoning with the many inequities present in society and also the relationships between people and the natural world. The teacher's efforts are justified by their desire to work toward a better future for all.

Justice-first science teaching aligns with the ideas of Paulo Freire (1970), who called for developing critical consciousness, an approach in which students learn to evaluate authority, question norms, and build diverse perspectives in order to fully understand their relationships and current position in the world. Once students have a critical lens and understand their social position, they can actively work to change the systems around them. Science provides a toolkit and a foundation for supporting these deeper critical aims.

DOI: 10.4324/9781003367192-2
This chapter has been made available under a CC-BY license.

Guiding Concepts

Figure 2.1 Education can empower young people to address social/ecological challenges

Justice-first science teaching also aligns with the ideas of bell hooks (1994), who argued that teaching must give full consideration to the ways in which student identity (e.g., race, gender, class) influence their position and future in society and also how those identities impact the depth to which the teacher and the classroom can be an effective space for learning. By explicitly considering identity, by encouraging active participation and vulnerability from both student and teacher, and by centering student experiences and questions, it becomes more possible to fully learn about the natural world and challenge human relationships to it.

2.2 Place-Based Teaching

Place-based teaching uses local places and associated phenomena to draw upon and guide scientific concepts, centering the learner's experience in inquiry (Sobel, 2004). It motivates students to engage with learning and develops their critical consciousness. By rooting science teaching in the natural world through local places, teachers can connect to students' experiences, identities, and values; frame learning from an asset-based perspective; and connect with

Guiding Concepts

Figure 2.2 Neighborhoods are meaningful places for student learning

issues and questions that are relevant to students' lives (Semken & Freeman, 2008; Stevenson, 2008). In turn, this engagement builds students' agency in their learning and in their communities, as their learning helps them create meaning and address challenges that are important to them. Place-based teaching provides students with a greater sense of academic agency, gives them opportunities to gain expertise, challenges their preconceptions around science, and improves their achievement (Rivera Maulucci et al., 2014).

Relph (1976) conceptualizes places as having three parts: (1) their physical setting; (2) their activities and events; and (3) their meanings, created through people's experiences. This means that students of different identities can experience the same place in different ways, as they each *do* things in the place and form *relationships* and *values* around the place. Place-based science teaching cannot focus just on the physical aspects of the natural world, but must embrace students' identities and lives, as well as history and society's impacts on them. In doing so, it can challenge these narratives Critical consciousness develops as students make sense of the natural world within the context of these three components of places and use their knowledge of the natural world to reimagine these places in the future.

Guiding Concepts

Place-based teaching can help combat student feelings of placelessness—what Relph describes as the creation of standardized landscapes that are insensitive to the significance of place. This can be particularly important for students who feel disconnected from their communities and to land, or who feel lost in the often-anonymous infrastructure of cities and suburbs, or who feel unable to make positive change in a world facing global-scale challenges. Many students are disconnected from these factors (Jack, 2010; Louv, 2008); they are disempowered by larger societal forces and implicitly told that they, and their places, do not have value, or power, or merit relationships (e.g., the erasure of Indigenous relationships to land; Bang et al., 2014).

Place-based teaching helps these students understand that their place, whatever it is, has value; it does not have to be "beautiful" or "wild" or "pristine" (Cronon, 1996); it can be found in an apartment courtyard, a warehouse sidewalk, or a fallow field. It teaches them that developing this understanding gives dignity and value to the place as well as to themselves. It teaches them that the possibility of repair and improvement exists (Taylor, 2021), and that unsettling ideas of who belongs to a place, and how it should be treated, can be a first step towards justice (Bang et al., 2014).

Figure 2.3 The built environment can contribute to feelings of placelessness

Situating teaching in place is an act of care and justice. It communicates to students that they, their homes, and their personal experiences are all important; that knowledge of these places is just as valuable as knowledge of other places; and that they are as valuable as people from other places (like they might see represented in a textbook or the media). Place-based teaching is an act of care and healing for the place itself—gaining understanding of a meaningful place, then potentially changing one's thinking or actions to help it. In developing this care, place-based teaching helps students understand their interconnectedness with their place, which in turn implicitly teaches them about their connections with other places and the natural world more broadly. Thus, place-based teaching can be important for supporting students of marginalized identities or communities because it returns power to them. It can also be important for Indigenous students because it recognizes and places value on the relationships between humans and the natural world, as well as around the deep meaning of particular places (Cajete 1999, Kimmerer 2013).

2.3 Inquiry-Based Teaching

Inquiry-based teaching invites students to learn how to frame their own questions about the natural world and then learn how to answer them. This approach centers students (MacKenzie, 2016), supports their development

Figure 2.4 Comparing insect behaviors on leaves in a schoolyard

of critical consciousness, and complements the goals of place-based teaching (Rivera Maulucci et al., 2014). Students can dare to ask any question and try to answer it. There is the possibility of transgressing against established power structures and the thrill of finding out something that no one else knows. That is, the desire for discovery and knowledge becomes situated with the student, in turn building a sense of agency and ownership. Inquiry allows students to ask scientific questions about the natural world so they can later ask related questions about their places and their society. Place-based inquiry is linked to land education broadly (Tuck et al., 2014), but the focus here is on scientific inquiry particularly.

Inquiry-based science teaching begins with exploration in places and builds from students' life experiences. This process then builds toward students creatively generating their own questions, whose answers are unknown, and transitions toward the design and implementation of a study in that place. Through the use of hypotheses and data generated by this process, students are able to engage in discovery at a local scale and make generalizations (test hypotheses) about the natural world. The knowledge they gain through this process is deeply rooted in the place they explored and studied. This knowledge helps them deepen their connection with their place and, most critically, change their mind, or others' minds, on the basis of evidence. Reasoning from evidence implies students learn to accept or reject an idea based on whether or not the idea is supported by data. This process allows students to develop a sense of humility and engagement regarding the process of generating scientific knowledge (Minner et al., 2010).

Inquiry-based teaching is based on constructivism (Marlowe & Page, 2005), which elicits students' prior knowledge and preconceptions, then engages students to build their own understanding through their own questioning. Benefits of inquiry-based teaching for students include more positive attitudes toward science and a higher interest in science careers (Gibson & Chase, 2002), greater proficiency with mathematics (Chen, 2013; Kjelvik & Schultheis, 2019), and improvement in science achievement including a narrowing of the achievement gap of historically excluded students relative to white students (Marshall & Alston, 2014).

2.4 Teaching Outside

Place-based scientific inquiry gains power when it is situated outsides. This change provides a connection to the natural world and a break from

Figure 2.5 Teaching outside expands the classroom to the natural world and society

indoor classroom teaching. It also validates the physical locations, actions, and meanings that exist for students outside the classroom. Teaching outside makes transparent the relationships and interdependence between people and the natural world that are obscured by living in an increasingly technology-dependent and urban society.

Teaching outsides contributes to developing critical consciousness. It causes students and teachers to confront the unequal access people have to the natural world that exists due to broader societal forces (urban development, feelings of being unsafe, violent dispossession) and the different priorities people have in their use of the natural world (e.g., for hunting or hiking or farming in a rural area, or for housing or parks in an urban area). Even if an inquiry has no explicit focus on land, students' values and access to the place remain important implicit components of the inquiry (Tuck et al., 2014).

Teaching outsides also contributes to justice-first teaching. It helps repair inequities by providing all students with safe and supportive access to the natural world, opening their lives to new experiences. Outdoor experiences provide a rich learning context for students (Louv, 2008; Riggs, 2005). Exposure to nature has positive psychological (Bratman et al.,

2015; Engemann et al., 2019), physiological (MacKerron & Mourato, 2013; Ryan et al., 2010), and social (Zelenski et al., 2015) effects and increases student interest in science (Zoldosova & Prokop, 2006).

2.5 Centering Student Identity

Justice-first teaching and place-based science teaching both require intentional consideration of students' identities. It is more effective to teach with this in mind than to ignore differences or pretend they do not matter in the classroom. Student-centered teaching must meet students where they are, follow them where they want to go, and respect where they have come from.

Identity indicates socially determined features that influence a student's access to power and resources. Frye (1983) uses the metaphor of being inside or outside of a birdcage to describe how each identity can position a student as being powerful or oppressed (e.g., via race/ethnicity, gender, or socioeconomic class) because they are either free to make choices or have their choices constrained (the birdcage). The way students are labeled by

Figure 2.6 Identity influences how a place is experienced

others thus shapes their life experiences, their understandings of how the world works, and their futures.

Identity matters in the context of place-based teaching because students' actions and meaning-making within a place are shaped by, and constrained by, their identities. Identity matters in the context of inquiry-based teaching because students' experiences and questions may be deeply informed by who they are. And identity matters in the context of outdoor teaching because access to outdoor places, and to land more broadly, is highly differentiated by identity; additionally, outdoor places are often designed in ways that implicitly teach students of some identities that they do not belong to, for example, Black (Finney, 2014) or non-white (Ho & Chang, 2021) people. Identity-based marginalization in these contexts can be addressed through justice-first teaching.

First, inquiry-based teaching can mitigate white supremacy culture. Leonardo (2009) argues that the white supremacy stems from prioritizing characteristics of whiteness as "normal." Anything that is not white becomes abnormal and grounds for discrimination and marginalization. Jones and Okun (2001) have highlighted several characteristics which are relevant in the classroom, including prioritizing the written word, claiming objectivity, promoting individualism, avoiding open conflict, believing in one right way, and assuming paternalistic authority. Inquiry rejects all of these premises. Also, including all students challenges the exclusion inherent to the construction of these outside places (Finney, 2014; Taylor, 2016).

Second, teaching outsides can combat marginalization of disabled students in the classroom (Baglieri & Lalvani, 2019; Jampel, 2018), who are often told that their minds, behaviors, or bodies are abnormal. Place-based inquiry centers students, removes barriers and norms common to classrooms, provides more diverse ways for these students to participate fully in learning, and enables them to reclaim their power and identity. Additionally, place-based outdoor teaching provides a foundation for integrating justice for disabled students with justice for land. Instead of discarding places that do not meet standards for "pristineness," these places are embraced as worth learning about; instead of describing places as degraded, they are described as harmed and worthy of care and repair (Johnson, 2017; Taylor, 2021). This viewpoint parallels how students are treated: instead of telling students that they do not belong in outdoor places, teaching is designed to embrace them with care.

Third, teaching outsides can draw strength from students' cultural identities (Gay, 2018). Because culture is partially grounded in the ways people use or value places, place-based inquiry provides a natural way for students to ground their learning, and their scientific inquiry questions, within their own cultural values, norms, traditional knowledge, beliefs, practices, and languages. The teacher's flexibility around questions and methodology allows for inclusion and belonging to develop for all students.

2.6 Meeting the Next Generation Science Standards

Place-based scientific inquiry closely matches key principles in the Next Generation Science Standards (NGSS) (National Research Council, 2012) and promotes an equitable classroom (Kolonich et al., 2018). This includes greater emphasis on student-led, open-ended inquiry instead of teacher-centered instruction. It also includes emphasis on questioning phenomena as a route toward discovering concepts and connections, instead of memorizing discipline-specific facts.

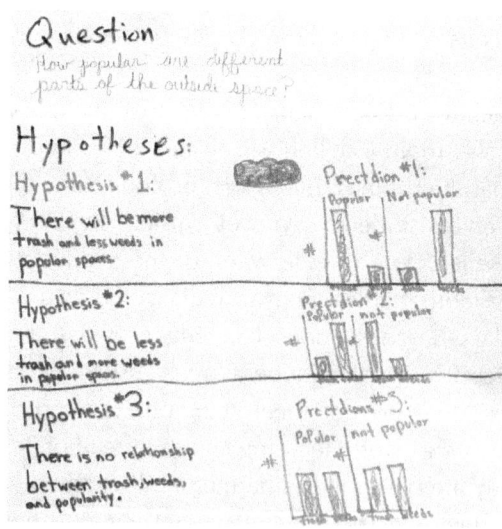

Figure 2.7 An example project conducted in a schoolyard that provides students experience with implementing the Science and Engineering Practices

The NGSS frame learning as three-dimensional, which reflects the idea that sense-making in science requires the inclusion and integration of three components:

1. Using specific Science and Engineering Practices that enable inquiry—that is, the behaviors that scientists engage in, utilizing discipline-specific skills and knowledge as they investigate and develop models and theories about the natural world.
2. Leveraging Crosscutting Concepts that provide a lens for students to understand scientific thinking—that is, the organizational framework of science that cuts across disciplines and provides a schema for a scientifically based view of the world.
3. Focusing on Disciplinary Core Ideas that are key for science education—that is, aspects of science that have broad importance or provide a key organizing concept in a single discipline, grouped into four domains: the physical sciences; the life sciences; the earth and space sciences; and engineering, technology, and applications of science.

The first two dimensions are integrated into place-based scientific inquiry; for the third, you can set the scope of an inquiry to cover the relevant Disciplinary Core Ideas.

The Science and Engineering Practices (Schwarz et al., 2017) support sense-making in place-based inquiry through the workflow of a project. Students naturally ask questions (Practice 1); create or use models to explain or predict phenomena, processes, or relationships (Practice 2); plan and carry out investigations (Practice 3); and then analyze data (Practice 4). Via analysis and graphing, they practice quantitative thinking (Practice 5) and construct explanations by comparing data to their hypotheses (Practice 6) and in doing so argue from evidence (Practice 7). Sharing results helps students obtain, evaluate, and communicate information (Practice 8).

Projects also explicitly address relevant Crosscutting Concepts. Observations in places prompt students to look for and speculate about patterns in nature, which they may confirm with systematically collected data (Concept 1). Many hypotheses will revolve around ideas of cause and effect or mechanisms that may explain patterns (Concept 2). Measurements require consideration of scale (Concept 3) and the factors influencing patterns (i.e., involving systems-thinking) (Concept 4). Most of the biological

Guiding Concepts

as well as physical processes students will explore outsides involve flows of energy and matter (Concept 5). Questions involving organisms implicitly include a relationship between structure and function (Concept 6) as the key result of evolution, and all biological and physical systems involve homeostasis and change (Concept 7). Most student-selected inquiry projects will draw on several of these Crosscutting Concepts.

Choosing the scope and location of your inquiry project, and thus the related phenomena to be studied using three-dimensional learning, will allow you to address specific Disciplinary Core Ideas. For example, you can take your students to a garden, park, plant nursery, or farm to encourage them to investigate plant life cycles; visit public lands or a local green space to observe interactions, energy, and dynamics in an ecosystem; or explore an open field, riparian area, or floodplain to make observations of the effects of weathering or the rate of erosion by water. Many of these phenomena can also be observed in your schoolyard.

More guidance regarding how to incorporate Disciplinary Core Ideas, Crosscutting Concepts, and Science and Engineering Practices in place-based inquiry projects can be found in Chapter 3.

2.7 Learning Beyond the NGSS

Our approach also supports teaching that goes beyond the goals of the NGSS. Inquiry projects naturally integrate with subjects like reading, writing, and mathematics—students read to find background information or determine the best methods to use; students write during observations and study design and as part of communicating their results; and students use mathematics to illustrate, analyze, and interpret their measurements.

Our approach also helps students to develop key skills—communication, team building, collaboration, creativity, problem solving, and flexibility—which will serve them throughout their educational and professional lives. Students thus experience learning happening not via isolated subject areas with a specific number of minutes designated each school day, but rather via integration of knowledge and skills from multiple content areas. This extends the philosophy and the evidence incorporated in the NGSS across all areas of learning in school and also supports development of place connection, responsibility, and humility in ways that are beneficial to students and society as a whole.

Guiding Concepts

Figure 2.8 Art complements observation

Students also gain a deeper understanding of scientific practices than is called for in the NGSS. Through inquiry, they discover that science is built from small, place-based questions and answers; that arguing from evidence often means allowing for uncertainty; that real-life measurements have substantial variation; and that humility is needed to interpret claims, even with evidence. Students also come to realize that multiple alternative hypotheses, creative study design, and peer discussion are needed to gain knowledge.

2.8 Decolonizing Teaching

Colonization is a process in which people in one society extract value and resources from people in another society, often leading to erasure of culture and places and harm to the natural world (e.g., the white settlement of North America involving violent land seizure and genocide against Indigenous peoples [Dunbar-Ortiz, 2014; Zinn, 2015]). Colonization also

Guiding Concepts

Figure 2.9 All places are worthy of care and are meaningful to those who live in them

involves shifts in knowledge, values, and norms that justify the legitimacy of the dominant society (e.g., via Western science).

Place-based teaching provides a key way to decolonize knowledge and narratives, working toward justice. Teachers can reflect on their (or their society's) curricular choices and their actions in the classroom, then re-envision alternatives. Reflection can focus on who has power in the classroom, whose stories are told, whose places are valued, and what societal futures are envisioned. Actions can focus on helping students to build relationships with their places, to take leadership roles as co-creators of knowledge, and to critically assess the narratives presented by their society. Similarly, decisions the teacher makes about how to structure the classroom can either reinforce or dismantle colonial norms. Dismantling begins with small actions—for example, a choice to let students co-produce knowledge and select their own inquiry question, a choice to develop students' conflict resolution skills, a choice to include all students with physical disabilities in outdoor activities, a choice to fully engage and learn from community partners, or a choice to use culturally responsive (Gay, 2018) or culturally sustaining (Alim & Paris, 2017; McCarty & Lee, 2014) pedagogies.

Place-based outdoor teaching supports decolonization. Such teaching cannot be separated from land and who has power over it (Tuck et al., 2014). Even apparently people-free or land-free inquiry questions (e.g., about rocks) make implicit assumptions about what questions are worth answering, who cares about the answers, who the rocks belong to, whether the rocks deserve care, and what right the person asking the question has to use the land to inquire about its rocks. Decisions the teacher makes around land are implicitly a choice either to support the dominant colonial narrative or to undermine it. For example, a choice to present a rural place to students as a "plantation" is a choice to not present its foundations of slave labor; a choice to present the "natural resources" in a forest is a choice to not present the place as having value beyond its economic potential; a choice to present a place as a people-free "wilderness" is a choice to erase the Indigenous use of the place (Cronon, 1996; Fletcher et al., 2021).

The apparent objectivity of Western science can sometimes reinforce colonial perspectives. Western science has been used to dehumanize certain people, to provide a justification for colonial society, or to disproportionately benefit scientists without collaboration with or benefit to local communities (Odeny & Bosurgi, 2022). In other cases, Western science has propagated a narrative of exploration and discovery (of places, of facts, of people) (Chakrabarti, 2017; Roy, 2018) that ignores longer histories of Indigenous people's presence and knowledge (Dunbar-Ortiz, 2014; Zinn, 2015) or has devalued key relationships between communities and place (Taylor, 2016).

Place-based outdoor teaching necessarily raises students' awareness of these issues because they are often omitted from traditional science teaching (Bang et al., 2014; Nxumalo, 2019). Decolonization is inherently uncomfortable because it requires envisioning, then enacting, substantial changes in the way society is organized and who has power within it (Tuck & Yang, 2012). Answers are not easy, but effective facilitation supports questioning.

2.9 Linking to Indigenous Science

Western science is one of many approaches to inquiry about the natural world that have been developed by human societies. The American educational system, as well as much of the Western world, currently privileges this approach to inquiry. Other approaches exist that provide different frameworks for valuing different types of knowledge, for making discoveries, for weighing evidence, for sharing knowledge, and for relating between people and the world. Because of the interdependence between people and nature, inquiry about the natural world is critical to every human society.

Decolonizing teaching requires considering multiple knowledge systems (Bang & Medin, 2010). Indigenous science is often neglected in the classroom. Indigenous approaches provide deep insights into the natural world (Kimmerer, 2013) and have enabled people to live more sustainably than in Western societies (Anderson, 2005). Recognizing Indigenous science can help Indigenous students better understand how their communities' knowledge systems are connected to Western knowledge systems, and vice versa for Western students, stimulating more inclusive and thoughtful perspectives from all students (Snively & Corsiglia, 2001).

There are some common perspectives in Indigenous science across cultures (Cajete, 2000). Some of these perspectives are complementary to the goals of place-based scientific inquiry. Place-based teaching supports the perspective of knowledge being situated in particular places, the importance of caring for connections between people and place (Basso, 1996), and the value of learning in high-context situations. Inquiry-based teaching supports the perspective that learners should have direct experience of phenomena and develop understanding through their own experiences, as well as the importance of experimentation and observation for making sense of the world. Outdoor teaching supports the perspective that connection with other organisms and the natural environment is intrinsically valuable. And justice-first teaching supports the perspective that science should benefit people and nature and that people have a responsibility to take care of the world. However, other aspects of Indigenous science (e.g., their relational and ceremonial aspects) are beyond this book's approaches (Smith, 1999; Wilson, 2008).

Teaching using the approaches in this book may help Indigenous students more fully and successfully participate in school-based learning because these approaches can affirm and support their knowledge systems (Cajete, 1999; Kant et al., 2018; Riggs, 2005). Additionally, recognizing and supporting multiple knowledge systems can help all students think critically about the societies they belong to, and which they may one day want to change, building critical consciousness. Honoring Indigenous perspectives is a first step (Jacob et al., 2021) toward envisioning wholly different curricula (RunningHawk Johnson, 2018) and societies.

 Setting Scope and Expectations

3.1 Your Role as Teacher

Concepts

Transitioning students from classroom teaching of content to place-based inquiry outside can be a challenge at first, both for you and for your students. For the students, expectations placed on their level of engagement and independent thinking will shift, especially if they are accustomed to rote learning, assigned projects with little choice, or learning about topics to which they feel no connections or relevance in their own lives. Place-based teaching allows you to center the student, although your role can also include providing student-led mechanisms to support assessment of learning in order to foster reflection and growth.

Equity and Inclusion

Even as you de-center yourself in the classroom, you should reflect on your own identity and positionality, because they will affect how you interact with students and how you connect with place and inquiry outside. Your life experiences and beliefs may resonate with some students and not with others; consequently, your ability to serve each student may also differ. There is no neutral position to start from in the classroom (Baldwin, 1963; hooks, 1994). A assuming that you are neutral effectively tells some students that they belong and others that they do not. By being clear with yourself about your starting point, you can become a more effective teacher.

Implementation

Place-based inquiry supports a transition to a student-led classroom. You become a facilitator of student development, supporting them in answering their inquiry questions. You may be accustomed to being the expert—providing facts, directing student activities, posing questions whose answers are known, and reaching set content points by set dates. However, this level of control means that students have little of their own control, and thus limited engagement. By becoming a facilitator, you share in students' discovery and agency.

Inquiry requires humility and an open mind about questions and outcomes of projects. You should provide opportunities for students to spend time in meaningful places, help them generate and answer their own questions, and help them critically reflect on what they have learned, without expecting them to reach any particular specific conclusion.

Being familiar with your own identity as it bears on the classroom is important. Key questions to ask yourself include:

- What identities do you have (e.g., race, class, gender, disability status, religion, age, level of education)?
- How are your identities similar or different from your students and people in the place you are studying?
- How do these identities influence who has and does not have power in the classroom?
- How do these identities support or challenge your teaching goals?
- What aspects of identity do you want to learn more about or be challenged on?
- What student identities or values do you imagine as being neutral?
- What would it mean for you to share your own identity and experiences in the classroom?

Being familiar with the identity of the place you are working with, and the identities of your students, is also important. Key actions to take include learning about:

- Who lives in, or has previously lived in, this place
- Social issues and history that have influenced the place

- Names of the place according to different groups of people
- Organisms or the environment in the place

You do not need to become an expert, but you do need to bring humility, care, an open mind, and a commitment to developing your knowledge base (e.g., see references in Chapter 2).

Grade-Level Differentiation

Elementary (3–5)

Students will ask questions easily but have more challenges with extended focus and teamwork. You can model respectful interaction styles.

Middle (6–8)

Students become more sensitive to being wrong or exposing their differences. You can model acceptance of others, showing curiosity about your own biases and discussing your identity.

High (9–12)

As noted earlier. You can encourage students to take more risks and responsibility for their learning, as well as to show their curiosity if they have been socialized to not do so.

Examples

Teacher positionality statement (co-author RL): I had educational opportunities upon my mother's insistence. My greatest privileges were being white growing up in an affluent Midwest suburb, though my family was lower income than most of my peers. My relationship to education as a student and then an educator has been influenced most by being a woman in science, a first-generation college graduate, a person experiencing disability, and a mother to two neurodiverse children. I strive to be an ally by challenging my thoughts, words, and actions, to reduce barriers for those who have been historically excluded from science.

Figure 3.1 Helping students observe a mullein plant

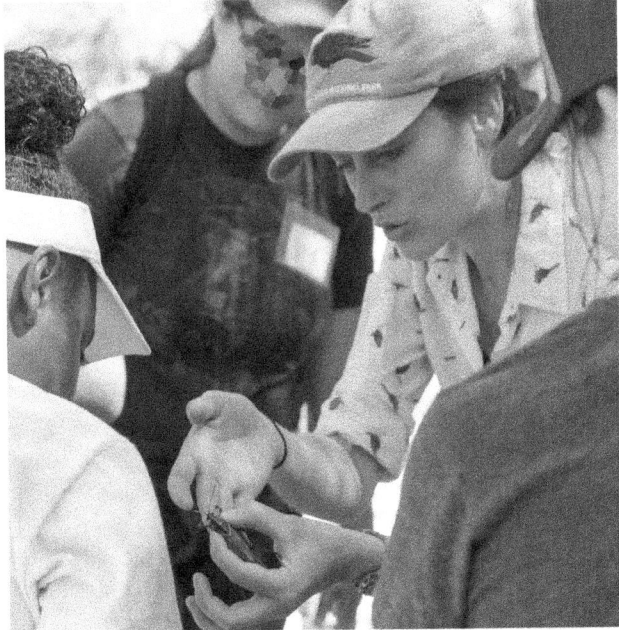

Figure 3.2 Helping students respectfully handle insects

3.2 Choosing a Topic

Concepts

It is tempting to structure students' projects in a way that results in pre-established answers. Projects without pre-established answers have more value because neither you nor the students know the answer (at least as it applies to this particular place and time). Discovery is possible, so learning becomes meaningful and students take on greater ownership of their project. Inquiry therefore must involve open-ended questions.

The specific conclusions that place-based projects reach have equal value to the process developed to reach them. Science is not only about learning content but also about learning the process of reaching that knowledge and developing one's interpersonal skills, curiosity, and responsibility to ask and answer questions about the natural world.

Equity and Inclusion

You can reflect on the following questions about your students (Kolonich et al., 2018):

- What funds of knowledge do your students have?
- What cultural knowledge do your students bring to their learning?
- What lived experiences have your students had related to this topic?
- Are there any "experts" on this topic in your school or students' communities?
- What language are your students used to or comfortable using in connection with this topic?

Implementation

Selecting the topic of an inquiry project can proceed in one of three ways.

First, you can focus content on particular Disciplinary Core Ideas appropriate to your grade level. For example, you can set expectations that projects must focus on a topic covered in the classroom in the last month, or you can tell students that their projects should relate to a particular subject area.

Second, you can let the content of an inquiry project be completely and freely determined by student interest. This approach provides the most ownership and flexibility to students but may be difficult to accommodate in your classroom.

Third, you can focus content based on the properties of the place you are working in or the stated needs of community partners you engage (see later).

In practice you can realize the first option by presenting a project to students via the second and third options, gently guiding the scope and topic of an inquiry through careful selection of the place the students can work in and the background information you provide. Students will still feel like they have free choice.

More topic focus also can be helpful if your students struggle with articulating their own questions or require additional structure, or if you are less comfortable with giving students full freedom of choice.

Grade-Level Differentiation

Elementary (3–5)

Independent topic choice requires more facilitation and guidance. More structure and less choice may be easier to facilitate.

Middle (6–8)

Independent topic choice is possible with additional support during the question and hypothesis generation steps. Small-group projects are feasible.

High (9–12)

Independent topic choice is possible. Small-group projects are feasible.

Setting Scope and Expectations

Examples

Figure 3.3 A nearby bridge supports inquiry around water-related Disciplinary Core Ideas

3.3 Scheduling and Time Considerations

Concepts

Longer projects have the benefit of allowing more careful and interesting investigations, deeper learning, more connection to place, and more student ownership of the inquiry process. They also require proportionally less transition times and introductory time, as students continue to engage with the same project and set of ideas over multiple meeting times. However, such projects may be unrealistic logistically if you have restrictive scheduling (e.g., short classes instead of blocks or students who have extracurricular obligations).

Shorter projects have the benefit of being achievable in a limited amount of time, giving you the flexibility to do other things in your classroom and to save money on equipment and transportation costs. Students may derive much of the benefit of a longer project from a shorter one, especially in terms of understanding the nature of science and developing process skills. However, short projects may feel stressful to both you and your students due to high pressure to complete an open-ended project in a limited amount of time. Additionally, many of the time costs of doing a project (e.g., facilitating group dynamics, forming hypotheses) do not change with the project length, so you will proportionately spend more time on introductory activities.

Equity and Inclusion

Students with Individualized Education Plans may require extended time or shortened assignments. Shortened assignments can be handled by expecting students to contribute to subcomponents of their overall team project, with assessment (if occurring) on only those components. Extended time is more challenging because longer access to places may not be logistically possible. Students can collect samples outside to analyze later in the classroom, take photos or video of a study area to refer to later, or refer to notes taken by their team. Assigning individual roles and tasks can help ensure project components are appropriate for each group member.

Implementation

Doing a project early in the school year equips students with skills and perspective they can build on later and may be used as a community-building activity, but students may also struggle without yet having a baseline level of trust among peers. Doing a project late in the school year maximizes their likelihood of success and can be a meaningful capstone, but minimizes the amount of time you can leverage success to achieve other goals. A late-autumn project is a good compromise for a first effort. However, you may also need to make the decision based on when a project of the selected topic matches your district's scope and sequence calendar. Environmental considerations may also be important: it may be too cold/hot/snowy for student safety or key phenomena may not be occurring (e.g., frozen ponds, hibernating animals, leafless trees).

A group of students on their first day of the year will not be ready for a long project because you still need to establish a culture of mutual respect. Team building (Chapter 6) can help. Similarly, a group of students who

Setting Scope and Expectations

have never learned outside of a textbook or multiple choice test may find the change in style and expectations daunting, so it is important to provide additional structure and guidance when getting started.

Sample project schedules are provided in Appendix 4. If you have full days or block scheduling, three part-day sessions are often sufficient for a shorter project that has a teacher-selected question, simple methodology, and does not rely on the development of a strong cohesive group. Five to seven part-day sessions or two to three full-day sessions should be sufficient for a longer project with more complexity or that requires closer collaboration between group members. If you have period scheduling, six to eight periods are a reasonable minimum for a shorter project. Chunk out project goals and timelines into manageable units (e.g., a single class period devoted to formulating a set of hypotheses, another to making a first set of measurements). Try to minimize transition times (e.g., by picking a site in the schoolyard that is a short walk from the classroom). Longer projects of ten to twelve sessions are hard to schedule but are the most rewarding, as students bond with their groups and build a sense of place.

Communicate to your students a clear timeline for the stages of the project (Which days will you be outside? When should a question be selected?). This helps both you and them with time management and expectations. In reality, plan for flexibility with some of these internal milestones depending on the group dynamics and multiple iterations of project design.

Plan to allocate your own time for several key pre-project tasks. Not all items will be necessary depending on the project scope.

6–12 weeks prior

- Choose and visit a place (Chapter 3)
- Gather background information (Chapter 3)
- Initiate community partnerships (Chapters 3 and 4)
- Acquire permits and consent (Chapters 3 and 4)
- Arrange transportation (Chapter 4)
- Acquire resources for students with special needs (Chapter 3)
- Submit trip forms for school (Chapter 4)
- Identify and recruit adult volunteers (Chapter 4)
- Conduct volunteer background checks (Chapter 4)

3–4 weeks prior

- Develop a risk management plan (Chapter 4)
- Acquire equipment (Chapter 4)

1–2 weeks prior

- Brief adult volunteers on expectations and roles (Chapter 4)
- Introduce inquiry project to students (Chapter 5)
- Communicate flow and stages of a project (all chapters)
- Communicate expectations for behavior, respect, safety, schedule, and assessment to students (Chapter 6)
- Communicate assessment plans (Chapter 14)
- Have students practice using equipment and recording data in the classroom (Chapter 9)

1–3 days prior

- Divide students into groups (Chapter 5)
- Distribute a packing list (Appendix 2)
- Order food from school cafeteria (Chapter 4)
- Arrange medications from school nurse (Chapter 4)
- Prepare equipment and other supplies (Chapter 4)
- Reiterate expectations
- Remind students how to prepare
- Organize all paperwork

Grade-Level Differentiation

Elementary (3–5)

Shorter blocks of time are better for shorter attention spans. Five minutes may be the longest students can focus on one area. Teachers may need to lead transitions to the next activities after a short time or provide extra guidance on retaining focus.

Middle (6–8)

Longer blocks of time and project durations are feasible. Longer projects can be empowering for students to feel ownership over their learning.

High (9–12)

Longer projects lasting over a whole semester (with more data collection and more sophisticated analysis) are possible. This will enable more accurate results, which in turn will make inquiry-based projects more useful for teaching not only the Science and Engineering Practices but also Disciplinary Core Ideas and Crosscutting Concepts.

Examples

The example projects in Appendix 5 each were done in 8–15 hours of time in groups of five to seven students with floating facilitation from a teacher, and with a single volunteer embedded with each group. This time included one hour of exploration and observations, one hour of question development, one to two hours of study design and methods development, two to six hours of data collection, and two to four hours of analyzing data, making conclusions, and preparing presentations.

Figure 3.4 Familiar places near school can support meaningful inquiry

Setting Scope and Expectations

Figure 3.5 Weather and seasons influence what features of the natural world can be studied

Figure 3.6 Transportation logistics (such as bus parking) can limit place selection

3.4 Scaffolding Projects into Your Curriculum

Concepts

Place-based inquiry projects can appear to have a time trade-off with your other curricular goals or classroom activities, particularly when extra time is needed for trips. However, such projects have direct and indirect benefits that can lead to a net gain of time and can help you scaffold learning towards your other goals. First, projects can cover multiple content standards, resulting in no direct loss of time. Integrating reading, writing, and math practice into inquiry projects promotes student engagement. Second, the Next Generation Science Standards (NGSS) are constructed to reduce the number of distinct disciplinary facts that students must learn, explicitly making space for student-led inquiry. Third, student-centered projects promote success by improving retention of material and increasing concurrent and future engagement in the classroom. In addition, developing students' place connections can help support further community engagement in other contexts. Direct experience with how science is done through the Science and Engineering Practices can deepen students' future engagement with scientific content.

Implementation

Decide which of your annual goals you want to focus on via place-based inquiry. For the NGSS, your choice of place will support developing student projects related to specific Disciplinary Core Ideas. Most Science and Engineering Practices and Crosscutting Concepts will naturally integrate into all projects. Then decide what other aspects of learning you want to explicitly address through linkages to students' projects.

You can combine inquiry projects with reading, reading comprehension, or background research on topics relevant to the project, or use writing assignments in which students summarize or interpret their own results or compare them with existing literature.

You can combine projects with teaching in social studies, history, government, or civics to support understanding and connection to place, as well as to support developing critical consciousness.

You can combine data analysis with a variety of math lessons, including practicing fractions, unit conversions, calculating means or other statistics, graphing, and generating and reading tables and graphs. These skills will gain in attraction and intuitive relevance when they naturally emerge from sense-making of their own data.

You can build on interpersonal dynamics. Students can be held to higher academic and behavioral standards after conclusion of the inquiry project. Some students can be more engaged during inquiry work than they are during regular classroom activities and show themselves capable in new ways. You can try to maintain this performance standard by reminding students of their past successes when they are back in the classroom.

You can build on place relationships. Students can extend components of their projects to longer timescales (e.g., repeated observations of a place, continued data collection) to deepen their understanding and connections. You can also use the place as a focal site or reference point for introducing other Disciplinary Core Ideas or Crosscutting Concepts (e.g., introducing ideas about the cycling of matter by remembering observations of leaf decomposition in a park).

You can build on community engagement. Students can extend their projects beyond the reflection stage to address a particular community need or justice issue. This can occur via community service, service learning (Kaye, 2004), or community activism (Oyler, 2012) approaches that support deeper engagement with the community based on findings.

Grade-Level Differentiation

Elementary (3–5)

Focus on integrating projects with reading, writing, and math, even while also fulfilling other goals. Use libraries or the Internet to find appropriate materials to share.

Middle (6–8)

Coordinate projects with other subject teachers to support synergies.

High (9–12)

As noted earlier.

Setting Scope and Expectations

Examples

Figure 3.7 Common Core math supporting a study of animal burrow locations

Figure 3.8 Developing environmental stewardship through studying and removing invasive grasses

3.5 Cost Considerations

Concepts

As projects expand in ambition, financial costs can also increase. You should set your expectations and project scope at a realistic level that matches the resources available. Categories of costs include:

- **Storage**—Backpacks, plastic tubs, bins.
- **School supplies**—Notebooks, pencils, whiteboards, paper, clipboards.
- **Equipment for data collection**—Thermometers, rulers.
- **Transportation**—School bus fees, public transit.
- **Permits and rentals**—Picnic area rentals, federal/state/tribal land access fees.
- **Food**—Snacks, extra water bottles.
- **Clothes**—Extra warm clothes, sun hats, socks.
- **Medical**—First aid supplies, medications, extra pads/tampons, bug spray, sunscreen.
- **Contributions to partners**—Gratuities, guiding services.

Equity and Inclusion

Passing these costs on to students (via mandatory parent/guardian contributions) is not recommended because of differences in families' financial situations. Fundraisers, donations, and grants are more equitable ways to obtain funds. If you do ask for parent/guardian contributions, ensure that they are optional and that opting out can be done without shame for either the student or parent/guardian and that contributions are distributed to equitably support all students.

Similarly, limit the expected items students should contribute because everyone may not have the financial resources or familiarity to obtain them. Whenever possible, budget for extra supplies.

If you are engaging community partners, offer to compensate them fairly for their time. Many partners will gladly donate time to schools; others will value financial support.

Implementation

Estimate a budget by category. Remember replacement and maintenance costs when students inevitably damage or break objects or use or lose consumable materials (especially pencils). Many equipment costs can be reduced by using zero-cost methods (Chapter 4). Other costs generally tend to be minimal. The biggest cost will often be transportation to an out-of-school location. If you cannot afford transportation, work in a local park or your schoolyard instead. Going farther does not necessarily make a project better.

Projects should only be implemented once appropriate resources are secured for all students.

Grade-Level Differentiation

Elementary (3–5)

There is less need to obtain complex equipment. Because students may be safest and most comfortable in a schoolyard, travel costs can be minimized.

Middle (6–8)

There is greater value from more complex equipment. Travel costs may be more valuable to budget.

High (9–12)

As noted earlier.

Setting Scope and Expectations

Examples

Figure 3.9 Even apparently featureless schoolyards hold surprises (here, earthworms) that can be studied with limited or no equipment

Figure 3.10 Neighborhoods near schools can be accessed at zero money cost and can be meaningful places to support observation and inquiry (here, a dead skunk)

3.6 Place Considerations

Concepts

Choosing an appropriate place is a balance between multiple factors. Critical considerations include:

- **Safety**—Your group should be able to work with a low risk of physical or emotional harm from natural or human sources.
- **Distance**—You should be able to spend most of your time engaged in teaching and learning rather than traveling.
- **Logistics**—Appropriate facilities should exist for your group (e.g., bathrooms, shade, tables).
- **Accessibility**—All of your students, including those with special needs, should be able to effectively learn at the site.
- **Permits**—Ensure that school groups are allowed and you have secured appropriate permission.
- **Ethics**—Ensure that your group's projects will be acceptable to landowners, members of the community, Indigenous rights holders, and other stakeholders.

Additional considerations include:

- **Content linkages**—Some sites have features that naturally align with Disciplinary Core Ideas (e.g., a pond if you are studying the water cycle).
- **Resonance and meaning**—By the end of their experience, your students should feel that the place holds meaning for them. You can choose a familiar place that may already hold meaning or one that may easily capture students' interest and care.
- **Durability**—Choose a location where you can minimize students' impact on the place (e.g., trampling/digging).
- **Contrasts**—A set of nearby locations can provide contrasts for students (e.g., city parks in poor and rich neighborhoods, meadows in fenced and unfenced areas, or streambanks and hill slopes).

Equity and Inclusion

Places do not have to be "pristine" to be meaningful and educationally valuable. Deprioritizing urban areas or environmentally harmed areas on these grounds can falsely indicate to students that they are not worthy of study, care, or repair.

Instead, prioritizing familiar or nearby places may better capture student interest. These places may also create a sense of protection from students or allow learning in the context of existing memories, experience, and expertise.

Be sensitive to multiple meanings a place may have for students, recognizing that your relationships and actions may differ from theirs. For example, some places may be sacred or otherwise not appropriate to use based on the beliefs of either your students or of community members.

Implementation

Brainstorm a list of nearby places, then use the earlier considerations to rule out inappropriate ones. Among whichever satisfy the critical considerations, most will likely be viable.

Think about your desired teaching outcomes, then about your logistical constraints (time, distance, group size), then seek input from city parks staff, federal/state/tribal land managers, tourism officials, or volunteers from local organizations (e.g., hunting/fishing groups, conservation groups, neighborhood associations, community activists).

Your schoolyard is a good candidate place. It meets all the critical considerations and is both familiar to students and a potential site that can be reinvented with new meanings. Even a large expanse of asphalt is full of materials and organisms and human activity that are viable subjects of inquiry.

Many developed recreation areas also offer sites that meet accessibility requirements.

In some places, you may need a permit for your group from the landowner or manager. Private land can often be used after obtaining verbal permission; city, state, federal, and tribal lands tend to have more formal processes. Be prepared to apply for a written permit and be able to wait a few weeks (or months) for approval. Frame your request in terms of its educational value and respect for place, as well as potential impacts. You will want to make a realistic estimate of potential impacts (e.g., total soil disturbance, total amount of biotic samples collected, total potential displacement of other land users). The likelihood of needing a permit is higher if the landowner or manager thinks that you may have a substantial impact on the land. Building relationships with these people can support you in revisiting the location multiple times during the year or in multiple years.

Review permit conditions to avoid causing damage. You may be restricted in the quantity of samples you can collect, or may have to avoid harming certain species, may need to avoid digging due to the presence of cultural artifacts, or may need to avoid trespassing on certain culturally significant sites. Taking these conditions seriously is a key part of stewardship and respect for place.

Grade-Level Differentiation

Elementary (3–5)

Working in a schoolyard will maximize student comfort and safety.

Middle (6–8)

Traveling is more feasible.

High (9–12)

As noted earlier. Consider having students engage directly with their neighborhoods. Students can participate in the place selection process based on their interests.

Examples

Figure 3.11 Schoolyards are accessible places to do inquiry with minimal costs

Setting Scope and Expectations

Figure 3.12 Local parks can have useful and accessible infrastructure

Figure 3.13 Culturally meaningful places can contextualize inquiry, like Heart of the Monster, a place central to the creation story of the Nimíipuu, the Nez Perce people. Students explored this place and learned this story before developing their projects

3.7 Student Identity Considerations

Concepts

Your goal is to help your students develop their interests and critical consciousness by building a connection with place. Students' identities may strongly shape each of these factors. Your own perspective may differ from your students, so it is important to step back and allow students to let their identities guide their interests, with you as a facilitator.

Equity and Inclusion

You have the power in the classroom to say "no" to students, to redirect or quash their interests. If you exercise this power, you are implicitly communicating something about the way power works and the (in)validity of their inquiry goals. Strive to help students shape their questions and interests into a doable project they can be proud of.

Implementation

Students of different identities may also have differing preparation and familiarity with asking their own questions, working in small groups, or being outside. You should encourage students to use their identities—for example, their family backgrounds, their lived experiences, their values, or their traditional knowledge—as valid starting points for observation, exploration, and question formation. This is particularly important for students whose identities are commonly marginalized in the classroom or in the broader society because they are not, by definition, often told their perspectives are valuable.

You should also necessarily open up, and support, the possibility of questions that address injustice. This may be true especially for inquiry questions with a strong human dimension (i.e., those that focus directly on people or on the relationships and activities occurring in a place). You should provide students the resources needed to pursue their interests and to facilitate respectful exploration of potentially controversial topics. No grade is too early to support age-appropriate inquiry around these topics.

There are several ways you can build a supportive culture that enables students to bring their full identities to their projects:

- **Avoid stereotypes**—Support all students in their interests without assuming what they might be.
- **Plan for cultural differences**—Educate yourself on cultural norms and traditions that may be relevant to your students in outdoor settings (e.g., objects that should not be touched, places that should not be visited, behaviors that are not appropriate).
- **Embrace place knowledge**—Consider working in places important to students. This information can be gathered from parents, local community members, and your students.
- **Invest in team building**—Take time for activities that promote positive group dynamics (e.g., team building and reflection, Chapter 6). Doing this throughout the project will help the rest go more smoothly. Make it safe for students to speak, contribute, and incorporate their identities and knowledge into their inquiry projects.
- **Establish and communicate guidelines**—Establish strong guidelines for safety and behavior expectations. Make explicit the implicit knowledge and expectations that you may have around working in small groups and outside. Leading the students in creating a group-designed set of behavioral standards can help to establish familiarity with, and ownership of, these principles and can be a team building activity as well.
- **Minimize barriers**—Reduce unnecessary barriers to participation (e.g., specific clothing items). Do not assume students have had particular life experiences (e.g., hiking).

Grade-Level Differentiation

Elementary (3–5)

Some students may not be fully aware of or able to articulate differences around identities, although you may be surprised at some of the ideas they already hold. Be prepared to ask clarifying questions and to help support

Setting Scope and Expectations

student explanations of their identities or perspectives to one another in age-appropriate ways.

Middle (6–8)

As noted earlier, students will likely have more developed ideas about identity, whether intentionally and culturally informed or absorbed from the media, family, and community. Be ready to address serious emotions from students as they confront some of these identity questions for the first time.

High (9–12)

Be ready to be surprised by what students do or do not already know or articulate, and keep a curious mind as you explore what they may mean by a statement. However, students are capable of nuanced conversations and diving into discussions of identity and may be eager to do so.

Examples

Figure 3.14 Providing space to reflect on place relationships while doing science. Here, students from the Pascua Yaqui tribe visit a mountain north of their home

Setting Scope and Expectations

Figure 3.15 Students may be unfamiliar or uncomfortable with environments different from their home (here, a sheep farm)

Figure 3.16 The potential for police or Border Patrol encounters outside the classroom can be especially stressful for students of marginalized identities

3.8 Universal Design, Special Needs, and Disability

Concepts

Framing the overall inquiry project from a Universal Design for Learning (UDL) perspective (Murawksi & Scott, 2019) provides a foundation for engaging all students (Baurhoo & Asghar, 2014). You can, and should, include all students in projects; all that is required is to plan ahead and consider ways that you can reduce or eliminate artificial barriers. Certain students with disabilities or Individualized Education Plans can be given additional support as needed. Strategies used to support students who are considered to need accommodations are often also beneficial to other students.

For students who are often excluded or limited in their participation in learning, engaging in inquiry projects outside can be especially resonant. The better you design your inquiry activities for all students, the less likely it will be that disabled students will need individual accommodations. Outdoor environments can promote positive engagement as students escape the confines of the classroom and find new ways to contribute and focus.

Your overall goal is to develop a community in which all students feel supported and valued. This is a conceptual shift away from the deficit-based thinking inherent to providing accommodations for students who are told they are not normal or part of a mainstream learning process, toward an asset-based model in which students' disabilities or other needs are key parts of their identities and a means of forming connection to place and doing inquiry. Students should be neither invisible because of their disability nor hypervisible.

Equity and Inclusion

Connection to place comes from relationships and actions, so it is important to be supportive of multiple ways of forming these relationships and multiple types of actions in a place. Outdoor sites are often constructed assuming they are for the use of able-bodied or white people (i.e., strongly indicating who a normal user should be). You could inadvertently teach many students they are abnormal by putting them in outdoor situations without providing appropriate care and resources. It can be difficult but important to challenge this assumption by finding ways for everyone to safely use these sites and help the sites to become meaningful places, despite structural barriers.

Implementation

Numerous strategies exist to support all students (UDL Principles 1–3) as well as particular students.

Principle #1—Provide multiple means of information representation (the "what" of learning):

- Include all students in outdoor learning.
- Use notebooks or graphic organizers for notes, data tables, vocabulary.
- Provide visual supports like photos, graphs, or diagrams.
- Provide background information at varying reading/language literacy levels.
- Consider barriers to students' comprehension, providing scaffolds and supports that will help students construct knowledge from new information.

Principle #2—Provide multiple means of student action and expression (the "how" of learning):

- Use assessment rubrics that recognize growth and skills development.
- Encourage students to show their learning in ways they are comfortable with (e.g., written language, drawing, symbols, photographs, video).
- Allow students to write in their preferred language when they are brainstorming or reflecting—any time there is not a need for others to understand what was written.
- Provide interim deadlines and regular check-ins for extended projects.

- Select a place that does not pose an undue burden on your students' mobility, or set expectations that going far or fast is not necessarily a priority. Some students will move at slower speeds, especially if you have picked a place that requires some walking or hiking. Do not single out students or groups that are moving more slowly than others. Instead, take regular breaks with the whole group to make observations, collect data, or do a sense of place or team-building exercise.

Principle #3—Provide multiple means of student engagement (the "why" of learning):

- Introduce projects from a perspective of team building and team success.
- Allow students to self-differentiate into teams focusing on different topics and preferred roles within a team.
- Have students come up with their own questions to pursue, even if the teacher provides an overarching topic.
- Make learning relevant to students' personal experiences and include ways to connect to their communities.
- Use team building activities to create a sense of community that draws students in and builds trust.
- Situate the student as an expert on their own project.
- Encourage a growth mindset by providing means to overcome obstacles to learning.
- Offer opportunities for self-reflection and self-evaluation.

Students with an Individualized Education Plan or a 504 plan:

- Review the accommodation and modification requirements for all students before beginning a project to ensure that students are serviced appropriately.
- Discuss with case managers how you can provide students with the necessary services without isolating or drawing unwanted attention. Guide the conversation by providing the case managers with information on the outdoor setting and team structure of the inquiry project.
- If a student is aware of their plan and their needs, find a private time to discuss the inquiry project expectations with them and/or include the student's parent/guardian.

- Students are protected by confidentiality, so do not discuss their needs with adult volunteers or community partners. Do direct them in how to best support the student.

Potentially marginalized students:
- Identify potential barriers that students may experience in outdoor places (e.g., mobility challenges, harassment by members of the public).
- Have conversations with students to explore the existence and origin of these barriers.
- Work together to identify actions the class and the student teams can take to mitigate these impacts during a project. Consider guiding inquiry questions or reflection directly towards these justice issues.

Neurodiverse students:
- Develop a plan in advance with the student and/or parent/guardian, along with the students' support team. Designate an adult the student can check in with if they are having difficulties and outline what options exist for them to be able to restabilize.
- Unfamiliar environments may be challenging for some students. Be aware of the sensory needs of students (e.g., bright sunlight or loud traffic sounds might be overwhelming). Make accommodations for students to comfortably participate (e.g., wearing sunglasses, using noise-canceling headphones, or choosing a quieter space) and be flexible with the ways in which students can comfortably participate.
- If a student uses social scripts, work with the student's support team to develop a script about this experience to prepare the student. A website with information about the location they will visit can help students know what to expect.
- Group neurodiverse students with peers and adults they feel comfortable with and who will be flexible and supportive of needs that arise.
- Identify a quiet place for the student to utilize if they become overwhelmed and need a break.

Setting Scope and Expectations

- Maintaining focus may be difficult for many students as they explore without close supervision. Speak with students in advance to set individual expectations before an inquiry project. Consider designing activities that provide a balance between focused work and free play.
- Do not make unnecessary behavior rules (e.g., students must stay seated), but do provide clear expectations with simple check-ins and specific goals. Allowing apparent chaos can actually support focus.

Students with physical disabilities:

- Navigating rough terrain may be challenging for students who use mobility aids. You can visit a place during the planning stage to identify easier-to-access areas. You can suggest dividing tasks within a group so that students who are managing mobility equipment can also handle samples.
- Consider finding adult volunteers to assist.
- Ensure that projects are designed with multiple modalities for engagement, including varied ways for all students to participate in peer discussions and the overall social milieu.
- Obtain assistive technologies (e.g., braille typewriters, screen readers, laptops) for students in advance as needed.

English language learners or American Sign Language users:

- Practice key vocabulary words with students beforehand.
- Request interpreters and prepare them in advance for any science vocabulary they may encounter.
- Bring visual aids.
- Encourage tactile engagement with the environment.

Blind/Low vision students:

- Blindness/low vision manifests in many different ways depending on the area of the eye affected, the progress of a degenerative condition, or the extent of an injury. A student's comfort outside may be different

than in the classroom due to variation in light level, terrain, and object motion.
- Provide orientation and mobility training for the type of environments students will encounter (e.g., uneven surfaces, loose rocks, tall grasses, dirt trails, mud).
- Obtain assistive equipment, such as talking sensors (e.g., talking thermometer) or magnifiers (e.g., cameras, tablets, smartphones).
- Ensure students bring assistive technology they already use in the classroom.
- Plan how all students will engage in the environment in ways that are inclusive of those who are blind/low vision to minimize special accommodations that set students apart (e.g., all students use magnifiers).
- Ensure all students who need sunglasses have them.

Examples

Figure 3.17 Tactile observation is an accessible approach that includes visually impaired students

Setting Scope and Expectations

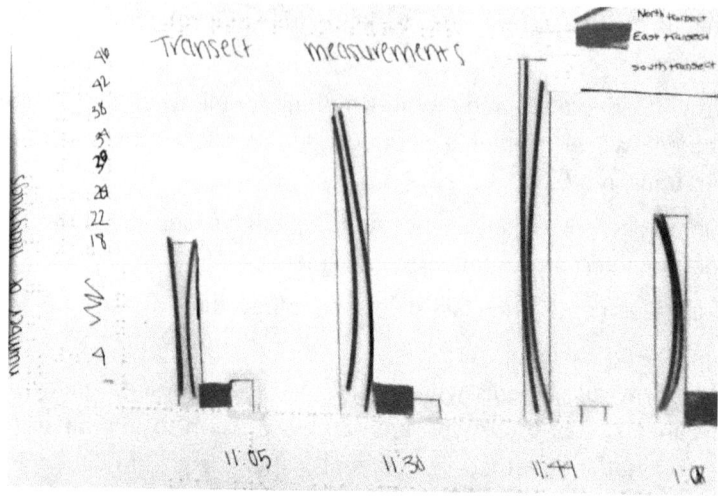

Figure 3.18 Tactile graphs can use embossed braille and textures (here, pine needles, colored sand, smooth glue)

Figure 3.19 An American Sign Language (ASL) interpreter supports hearing impaired students

 Acquiring Resources and Planning Safe Logistics

4.1 Partnering with Volunteers

Concepts

Additional adults can help manage logistics and safety and facilitate student work in small groups. This is especially valuable for maximizing your ability to circulate between groups as a facilitator and for reducing student group size.

However, using volunteers may have downsides. Volunteers need to be recruited, trained, and managed, which also requires time. Volunteers may also need to pass a background check, which can be slow. Volunteers may try to take a too active role within student groups if they find themselves motivated by the inquiry project, taking agency away from students.

Teachers' aides, student teachers, or community-based volunteers are ideal volunteers.

Equity and Inclusion

Care must be taken when recruiting parents/guardians, as some students will not have someone available to volunteer, which could be embarrassing to or disadvantage them. Community volunteer organizations with relevant missions may be better partners (e.g., around outdoor experiences, park stewardship, corporate/retiree community service). Their volunteers may

DOI: 10.4324/9781003367192-4
This chapter has been made available under a CC-BY license.

be able to spend time that parents/guardians do not have available, especially for schools with fewer resources.

Volunteers may communicate damaging stereotypes or ideas about learning to students. They also may interfere with student learning by too quickly offering solutions or suggestions to students, thus hampering students' creativity, confidence, and problem-solving ability. Setting clear expectations for volunteers is critical.

Parents/guardians may complicate group dynamics by favoring or disfavoring their child over others. Students should not work directly in small groups with their parent/guardian unless specific support is necessary (e.g., health needs).

Implementation

Recruit volunteers through your school or community organizations. Provide volunteers a clear set of expectations about scope (location at the school and/or focal place, how many hours), accessibility, and responsibilities. Ensure they agree to your expectations before accepting them. Consider also holding a pre-project meeting with volunteers to set norms and answer questions. You can ask whether volunteers have particular skills to offer (e.g., language skills, medical training, place knowledge).

Standard practices around child welfare should be followed (e.g., no lone contact between students and volunteers, all out-of-school communication with students must include parents/guardians).

Volunteers do:

- Ensure students are physically and emotionally safe in their groups
- Spend multiple hours outside while walking
- Assist with carrying equipment, notebooks, and safety gear
- Help facilitate positive discussion and interactions between group members
- Keep groups on task and on schedule
- Communicate issues regularly to you, the teacher
- Provide positive feedback to students

- Help students carry out measurements and other activities
- Ask open-ended questions with appropriate wait time
- Provide culturally competent support to students of all identities
- Follow all other school policies (e.g., around photography)

Volunteers do not:

- Tell students how to carry out their project
- Provide answers to questions that students should answer
- Analyze data for students
- Take measurements when a student could more appropriately carry out the work
- Distract students through unnecessary technology use
- Make assumptions about students based on their identities
- Single out their children

Be mindful of volunteer needs. If projects involve walking substantial outdoor distances, volunteers with limited mobility or low physical fitness may be more comfortable in the classroom. When developing a risk management plan, consider hazards not only to the students but to volunteers (e.g., increased hazard of cardiac events for older adults). Ensure volunteers are given a packing list (Appendix 2).

Volunteers should be introduced to students early in the project to build trust and relationships.

Volunteer expectations and limits must be clearly defined and communicated, as along with a policy for failing to meet expectations. A volunteer who is consistently not benefitting students or meeting agreed expectations should be excluded from further participation.

Grade-Level Differentiation

Elementary (3–5)

Volunteers are especially valuable for supporting student focus and emotional well-being.

Examples

Figure 4.1 A county employee provides guidance to students working in a regional park, with American Sign Language (ASL) interpretation

Figure 4.2 Members of a local environmental organization loan binoculars and provide support for a bird observation project

Acquiring Resources and Planning Safe Logistics

Figure 4.3 An adult provides supervision and support to a student team

Figure 4.4 Community members prepare a warm fire and lunch for students working outside

Figure 4.5 Volunteers (left) can carry equipment and provide options to handle outdoor safety incidents if they arise

4.2 Acquiring Equipment and Collecting Data at Low Cost

Concepts

Inquiry projects often require equipment to collect data. You may not have this equipment available or the money to purchase it. Or, you may not know what equipment is even needed to collect the data or how to use it. These apparent barriers can often be overcome without spending money.

Understanding available resources can help structure students' thinking as they design their projects and also teaches students about planning around real resource constraints that exist for projects outside the classroom. Even a relative scarcity of tools can feel like an abundance to a student unaccustomed to freedom of choice in school. Limitations in equipment options can also generate creativity in designing questions and approaches.

Equity and Inclusion

Inclusive projects can often be done with lower-cost equipment. Many districts have science resource centers that can help with basic equipment needs. Mini-grants or Internet donation platforms can also help to secure funds when needed. Students' parents/guardians should not be solicited for funding.

Implementation

Useful equipment can be made from low-cost, easily purchased objects.

- **String/rope**—Used to label/bundle objects and to measure distances/lengths of irregular objects (e.g., tree diameters).
- **Measuring tape/meter stick**—Used to measure lengths.
- **Level**—Used to measure slopes utilizing geometry.
- **Ice cube trays**—Used as a set of miniature compartments to store different things (e.g., plant clippings, aquatic insects, and water samples).
- **Cups/envelopes/sealable plastic bags**—Used to hold larger objects that do not fit in an ice cube tray (e.g., to collect soil samples, larger plant clippings, larger insects).
- **Plastic vials**—Used to collect water samples or small objects.
- **Trowels**—Used to dig small holes.
- **PVC piping**—Used to make quadrats (four straight sections with elbow fittings make a square).
- **Magnifying lens/tweezers**—Used to view and manipulate small objects.
- **Kitchen/luggage scale**—Used to measure mass.
- **Kitchen timers**—Used to measure time intervals (e.g., for estimating speeds).
- **Kitchen thermometers**—Used to measure temperatures.
- **Oven**—Used to dry an object (e.g., for dry mass). Use low temperature to avoid starting a fire. Foil cupcake liners can be used to hold samples.
- **Paint sample booklet**—Used to assign a value to colors.

Smartphones can also be used in scientific inquiry and are frequently available. As long as one student within a group has one, measurements can be made. Possible measuring/recording uses include:

- Timing
- Identifying species
- Taking photos/videos
- Recording audio/interviews
- Measuring sound/light intensity
- Estimating distances and heights (e.g., trees, buildings)
- Sensing the environment (e.g., air temperature, humidity, dew point)

Free apps can be found for all of these purposes.

Human senses allow measuring length, color, light level, temperature, moisture, texture, sound, smell, taste, and many other features of the natural world. You can develop qualitative scales for each sense (e.g., for sun light: dark, dim, bright, very bright) and calibrate them by having multiple students measure the same thing until they reach consensus. Alternatively a single student can make all measurements to avoid interstudent biases.

The human body can also be used as a length scale. A student's body part can be used as a standardized length unit and later converted back to standard units. For example, a tree diameter can be measured in units of hugs, or a rock length can be measured in units of thumbs.

Some equipment can be built using low-cost supplies. Internet searches can yield plans for homemade versions. Students may learn as much from building their own equipment as they do from carrying out their projects.

You can also ask to borrow equipment from nearby universities, community colleges, government agencies, or corporations. Identify specific people (e.g., a faculty member or a manager) and then ask whether they have what you need or know someone else who does. Alternatively, your volunteers or students' parents/guardians may be able to provide ideas and connections.

Grade-Level Differentiation

High (9–12)

Students can help by researching smartphone or homemade methods for measurements, or they can reach out to potential partners to request equipment.

Acquiring Resources and Planning Safe Logistics

Examples

Figure 4.6 Storing samples in plastic cups and sauce containers

Figure 4.7 Drying samples in aluminum tins using a kitchen oven

Acquiring Resources and Planning Safe Logistics

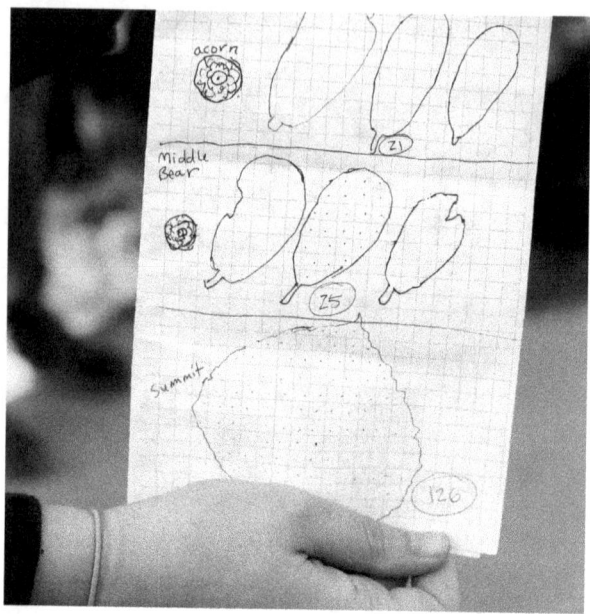

Figure 4.8 Measuring leaf area by counting squares on graph paper

Figure 4.9 Examining stream macroinvertebrates using spoons and a plastic tub

Acquiring Resources and Planning Safe Logistics

Figure 4.10 Observing insects using an inexpensive magnifier bought on the Internet

Figure 4.11 Making observations by licking and smelling a tree

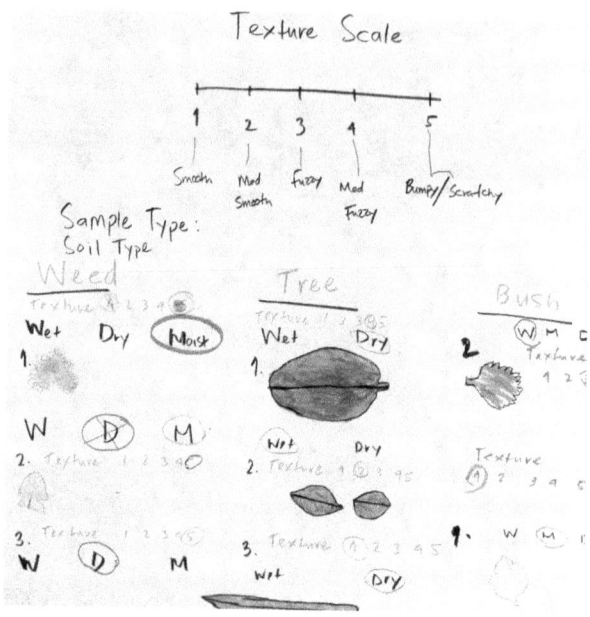

Figure 4.12 Collecting texture data by rating leaves on a 1–5 scale

Figure 4.13 Collecting carbon flux data using a gas analyzer borrowed from a university

4.3 Safety and Logistical Preparation

Concepts

Teaching outside, whether in the schoolyard or in more remote sites, brings additional safety considerations. Safety should be considered both from a physical perspective (e.g., dehydration, car collisions, lightning) and an emotional perspective (e.g., harassment from the public, bullying from peers, exposure to complex social issues). Be aware of likely hazards, making sure to review identity-based risks including accessibility needs. Writing and implementing a risk management plan can help you identify and plan for potential safety issues.

Teaching outside also brings additional logistical considerations. Objects and resources you are used to having on hand (e.g., bathrooms, extra paper/pencils) may not be readily available unless you plan ahead for them. Similarly, students and volunteers may not be able to meet their own needs if they do not bring necessary objects with them.

Equity and Inclusion

Students' identities may play a key role in determining a project's risk, for example, if you are bringing non-white students to a primarily white community where they may be harassed, or if you are bringing students who do not have experience interacting with farm animals to a place where they may interact with them, or if you are asking students who have limited physical to climb a mountain. Make sure to consider identity-based risks when doing a risk management plan (Appendix 2).

Students may end up engaging with complex social issues when working in outdoor places (e.g., houselessness, pollution, public drug sales). For some students, this may be their first time encountering the issue, while for others, the issue may have personally affected them or their community already. In either case, there may be strong emotional reactions. Engagement can therefore be considered a hazard; mitigation can involve using facilitation strategies, classroom-based learning, or dialog with community partners to promote respectful discourse, giving advance warning of what to expect, and/or giving students opportunities to take a break if needed.

Acquiring Resources and Planning Safe Logistics

For students, being outside is potentially a novel and stressful experience where emotional or physical discomfort is possible and where their expectations from the classroom are challenged. To improve this aspect of safety, you should consider:

- **Communicating expectations**—What the weather will be like, how long the bus ride is?
- **Providing discreet access to additional supplies**—Water, menstrual products, sunscreen, toilet paper, Band-Aids.
- **Facilitating basic needs**—Indicating location of toilets and taking breaks while walking.
- **Communicating schedules**—When it is time to take a break, to have lunch, and to go home.
- **Normalizing having needs**—Running through scenarios in the classroom may help students understand how to communicate their needs.

To give students tools to articulate what they are experiencing and to decide what they need, define and contrast the comfort zone (not a challenge), the growth zone (students are challenged but motivated to work through a challenge and grow), and the danger zone (students are challenged to the point of being overwhelmed or unsafe, and should step back).

Implementation

Visit the place before taking students to it. During this visit, think about potential hazards (e.g., traffic, falling hazards), general accessibility (How far must students walk? Over what type of terrain? How does that match with their ability levels?), and the available facilities (Where will students use the bathroom? Can they find shade to cool off or shelter to warm up? Is there drinkable water? Are there tables to work on?). Sometimes it may not be possible to pre-visit a distant place. In this case, contact an employee at the place to review these questions.

Write and then implement a risk management plan (Appendix 2). Some specific safety considerations include:

- **Information**—Obtain and carry appropriate documents in case you need them (e.g., medical forms for all students including

allergies, phone numbers for local emergency services and/or land managers).
- **Communication**—Bring communication tools that work at the place (e.g., mobile phones). If cell phone signal is intermittent or groups are spread over large areas, consider two-way radios. A satellite beacon is a good—but expensive—communication option if you are in a remote location. If none of these are available, have a default meet-up location and time planned.
- **Medical situations**—Identify the first aid kits you have, who will carry them, who is trained and allowed to provide first aid, and what injuries are beyond your treatment capacity. In the event transportation to a medical facility should be required, plan who will take the student and who will remain with the rest of the group to facilitate. You should have at least one other adult with you so you can maintain leadership while a situation is resolved.
- **Boundaries**—Set clear expectations for traveling and working as a group. Explaining the rationale for these expectations can help improve student compliance (e.g., "I am asking you not to swim in the creek because you may be swept away" or "I am asking you not to throw rocks because you may hurt someone"). Students should stay within eyesight of an adult at all times and should not work alone. When traveling from one place to another, particularly when crossing roads or parking lots, groups should stay together. Students who are lost should stay in place until found.
- **Facilities**—Being outside limits the infrastructure and resources you will have on hand. If you are working somewhere without bathroom facilities, be prepared to teach students how to safely and hygienically relieve themselves. Some students may dehydrate themselves to avoid peeing, so provide appropriate training, supplies, privacy, and norms before going outside. Humor surrounding physical practices can help reduce the awkwardness students may have at first. Share Leave No Trace principles (1987) and make space for questions and discussions.
- **The public**—Students may interact with members of the public who may be curious or have bad intentions. Prepare students in advance by asking them to say, "I am working on a science project with

my school." Students should keep interactions with the public short. You should be aware of people from outside the group approaching students and have an adult nearby to assist if needed. If you are concerned about harassment by the public, the police, or other authorities, consider having students wear clothing identifying them as members of a school group.

- **Accessibility**—Students need to be able to not only work safely in a place but also leave it quickly in an emergency. Ensure that students with mobility limitations or communications-related needs are also able to be contacted and evacuated quickly if necessary. Be sure to check in with students in advance about what options and accommodations work best for them. Be ready to be flexible and change plans as needed.

Also make a logistics plan. This plan should include:

- **Transportation mode**—Walking and public transport are low-cost and simple options but limit the amount of equipment you can bring. Fifteen-passenger vans work well for relatively small groups and allow space for extra equipment. School buses work well for larger groups with more equipment but can be costly and are potentially unable to access some places due to vehicle size.
- **Equipment**—Bring all needed research equipment, especially if your classroom is inaccessible from your study location. Enlist the help of students by dividing responsibility for carrying and caring for gear.
- **Extra supplies**—Consider bringing extra materials as backups, including extra pencils and notebooks, clothing for students, personal hygiene supplies, etc.
- **Weather**—Check the forecast before you go and ensure students are adequately prepared. Or decide not to go if conditions warrant; it is better to be delayed than unsafe.
- **Packing lists**—Make a list of items students can realistically bring which will improve their comfort and safety. Sample lists are in Appendix 2.

Grade-Level Differentiation

Elementary (3–5)

Communicate any emergency plans in a simple, clear manner to students. Establish rules even for things you consider obvious (e.g., nothing found is to be eaten without permission).

Middle (6–8)

As noted earlier. Also consider the hazards of students intentionally sneaking off from the main group.

High (9–12)

As noted earlier. Also share risk management plans and make sure students know where to find safety equipment.

Examples

Figure 4.14 Appropriate clothing keeps students comfortable in the rain. One student is wearing a trash bag to stay dry, a non-ideal and improvised solution

Figure 4.15 Setting space-use boundaries can prevent accidents like falling

Figure 4.16 Eye protection when using hammers

Acquiring Resources and Planning Safe Logistics

Figure 4.17 Some natural objects may be tempting to eat, like these poisonous red-colored coral bean seeds (which are also used widely as beads)

Figure 4.18 Fast-moving and murky water is hazardous

Acquiring Resources and Planning Safe Logistics

Figure 4.19 Traffic and street crossings are key hazards to consider

Getting Started via Exploration and Team Building

5.1 Dividing Students into Groups

Concepts

Students should work in small inquiry groups. Small groups allow skill sharing, division of labor, and building of teamwork skills, as well as exposure to the diverse perspectives and place relationships of teammates. Dividing students into groups also reduces the amount of time you spend facilitating and assessing projects. Smaller groups support more student agency than larger groups.

Equity and Inclusion

Stratification of students into groups can have racist and ableist undertones (Leonardo, 2009). Students are sometimes placed in a group based on perceived intelligence and arbitrary expectations around behavior. This may lead to certain students becoming isolated or limited in their access to learning. Students should not feel that their identity or academic performance placed them in a group inequitably or that they were singled out. Consider simpler methods of grouping like randomization or affinity (e.g., a rock group and a plant group).

Implementation

Groups of five to six students are best. In a typical 30-student classroom, this yields five to six total groups. For students, this size allows each person to have clear roles and responsibilities, while not being too large and unwieldy for collaboration. For you, this size yields few enough groups that you should be able to circulate to facilitate. A lot depends on how familiar students are with working independently and thus how much supervision might be needed for each group.

If groups are too large, then students may not have clear roles, and participating in group decision-making can be difficult, leading to learning and behavior challenges. If you have a large number of students, try to get additional adult volunteers to help with facilitation so you can keep groups small. If groups are larger, be prepared to spend additional time facilitating each group and/or lower your expectations for active participation of all students. Alternatively, if you have limited facilitation capacity, consider doing a single whole-class project where you help all students through the inquiry process together and multiple students work together within roles.

Grade-Level Differentiation

Elementary (3–5)

Consider doing a single whole-class project, or have multiple groups do the same project. This reduces the number of logistical challenges, allowing you to assist students better in moving forward on their project. A trade-off is that you have to invest more time in ensuring each student knows what their task is and remains engaged.

Middle (6–8)

Start with small-group interactions in predesignated teams, then allow students to keep their work group. Or split into triads, then have each triads find another triad to make groups.

High (9–12)

As noted earlier.

Getting Started via Exploration and Team Building

Examples

Figure 5.1 Students sorting into teams based on interests (indicated on sheets held by adults in foreground)

5.2 Using Notebooks

Concepts

Inquiry notebooks can support learning. They can be used to make observations, write down protocols, record data, make journal reflections, and take other notes (Fulton & Campbell, 2014). Having a notebook provides a single location for students to engage with the project, distinguishes the project from classroom worksheets, and gives students a sense of ownership over the process. Having a notebook also can create a useful artifact of the learning process that can be assessed using rubrics (Chapter 11) or be shown to parents and administrators.

Equity and Inclusion

Some students may have less experience using an inquiry notebook. Try to provide high-quality examples once you have prior work on hand, and allow students within groups to use notebooks in different ways (one student may write down more observations, while another may write down more data and another may draw more diagrams or pictures).

Implementation

Any blank notebook will work, although lined or graph paper can be helpful for organizing data. You can help set up notebooks in advance by labeling sections you plan to use (e.g., Observations, Data).

You can make inexpensive homemade notebooks by taking some sheets of copy paper, folding them in half, then stapling them in the middle. You can have students write their name on the cover page. Adding a cardboard backing improves students' abilities to write outside and prevents crumpling in backpacks. Students will need 10–20 notebook pages for a long project or 5–10 for a shorter one.

If available, tablets or laptops can also be used as notebooks. This can be useful for students with poor handwriting or for students with Individualized Education Plans and can make data sharing easier. However, challenges may occur outside if you experience inclement weather or do not have access to electrical power.

Grade-Level Differentiation

Elementary (3–5)

Consider handing out and collecting notebooks at the end of each day to prevent them from being lost or damaged in backpacks. You can optionally attach a pencil to each notebook with a piece of string and masking tape to prevent loss.

Getting Started via Exploration and Team Building

Examples

Figure 5.2 Drawing three views of a landscape

Figure 5.3 Making observations of whether ants prefer eating pepperoni or bread

Getting Started via Exploration and Team Building

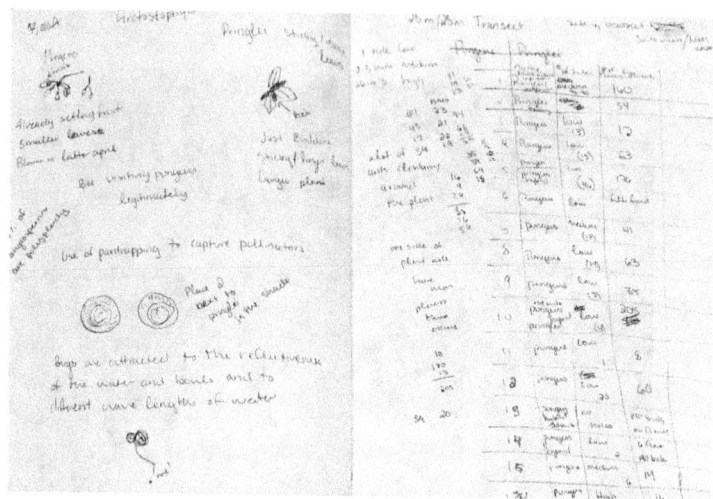

Figure 5.4 Taking notes and recording data

Figure 5.5 An observation of a duck that apparently has four legs. Teaching observation skills is critical for effective notebook use

5.3 Exploration, Observation, and Sense of Place

Concepts

Exploration and observation are critical to building place connection. It is easier to care about ideas and places that students know than those they do not. These places, which are not controlled classroom environments, provide learning opportunities and ways to motivate inquiry.

Observation is a critical activity before inquiry because it promotes connection to the actions, objects, and relationships that characterize a place and provides a foundational level of knowledge and engagement that can stimulate question formulation.

Exploration and observation are closely related. Exploration builds emotional connection to place; observation is a tool that can generate emotion, but also knowledge. Together they build a sense of place (Kudryavtsev et al., 2012; Semken & Freeman, 2008) and provide students the foundational motivation and knowledge to begin to identify a question.

Equity and Inclusion

Decoupling learning from local communities and local concerns can alienate students. Rooting your teaching in a sense of place, examining local phenomena and utilizing familiar examples, provides a key foundation for effective learning. The fabric of a city; the opinions, struggles, and behaviors of its people; and the challenges facing its natural environments are all valid and important subjects of inquiry. It is important that you communicate care and curiosity about all places to your students, especially if they do not fit the stereotype of people-free nature.

Implementation

Provide time for students to freely explore and interact with a place, making sure they are prepared to be outside (packing lists are provided in Appendix 2).

Even if the place is familiar (e.g., the schoolyard), students may come to see it differently if you prompt them appropriately or if you give them the opportunity to spend unstructured quiet time in the place.

You should model a respect for the places students are working in, as well as a personal curiosity for them. By setting a good tone, you will encourage positive interactions of students with the place. Some strategies for doing this include drawing on student life experiences in places—ask questions that allow students to scaffold on their prior experiences in a place, for example, "What did you notice about X when you came here before?" or "What does X mean to you?". Alternatively, you can have your students observe or reflect on the different groups of people who might use a place.

Include sense of place activities throughout the inquiry process, but especially at the beginning. Do not skip these activities to save time—a strong sense of place can develop student interest in ways that shape their inquiry projects and build long-term engagement. The novelty of spending school time on such activities may also help some students widen their perspectives on what the boundaries of school learning can be and may also help students come to a new appreciation for their local places.

You should introduce students to the type of equipment that is available to them and discuss its possible uses. If you have a box of supplies, let students play with them during the exploration or methods stage of the project. For observation, sensing equipment is especially valuable. Examples include thermometers, sound meters, pH test kits, and color wheels but also art supplies like crayons, molding clay, and cameras.

Visual

- **Human place use**—Students observe how other people use the place for five minutes. Take notes on who the people are, what they are doing, and how long they stay.
- **Animal place use**—As noted earlier but for an organism.
- **Close observation drawing**—Students draw a small scene as carefully as possible for five minutes. Share drawings with another student and see if they each noticed something different.

- **Paired drawing**—Students in pairs stand back to back. One student describes what they see to the other who then draws it. Then exchange and repeat in the other direction. At the end, both students exchange drawings and see how accurate they were.
- **Natural history notes**—Students choose an object to draw/diagram. Use arrows to label parts, and include notes about the date/time, conditions, etc. (Laws & Lygren, 2020).

Auditory

- **Sound map**—Students pick a place to silently stay in for five minutes. Any sound they hear in front is drawn on the top of the page; to the left, on the left of the page, etc. Sounds can be drawn as cartoons or words, with distances from the page center proportional to the distances from the observer. Discuss unexpected sounds and unique sounds that only one student heard.
- **Sound inventory**—Students use a smartphone to make three- to five-second sound recordings of interesting phenomena at different locations in the place. They then share the story of why they chose their particular recordings.
- **Interviews**—Students talk to members of the public in the place. They ask questions about what the person is doing in the place, how the place has changed, or what they enjoy about the place.

Tactile

- **Natural art**—Students collect materials such as twigs, leaves, or pointed rocks. Have them build a sculpture, make a painting, or imagine building a home for an animal using the objects. Then return objects to their original locations.
- **Tactile exploration**—Each student collects one object from the site such as a leaf or a stone. Have students sit in a circle and close their eyes. Ask them to explore the object with their hands, feeling its texture, shape, and size. Have students pass their object to the left or right and repeat the exercise with an object they did not collect. Students can write their observations in their inquiry notebook or share them out loud.

- **Meet a tree**—Divide students into pairs: one blindfolded, one not. The first student disorients the second blindfolded student by spinning them around and walking them to a nearby tree. The second student is given time to touch/smell/taste/listen to the tree and is then walked to another location and disoriented further. After their blindfold is removed, the second student tries to identify the tree they met based on the evidence they obtained while blindfolded. The tree can optionally be identified using a guide afterwards. Student pairs then switch roles (Cornell, 2015).
- **Color rainbow**—Students find objects of as many colors as possible or of as many shades of the same color as possible. They can take photos with their phone camera or, if ethical, temporarily collect the objects to make a rainbow before putting them back (e.g., autumn leaves).
- **Circle observations**—Students work in pairs to list as many observations as they can about an object, then they pass their object and paper to the next pair, who adds more observations, until each object has made it all the way around the circle. This becomes more challenging for each pair as they are pushed to be more detailed and creative about their observations. Have magnifiers available for students to use.

Writing

- **Guided poem**—Students write their name in capital letters down the left side of the page. For each letter, write a line of a poem starting with that letter about the place.
- **Free write**—Students write about whatever comes into their mind as they sit in a place, not stopping if the mind blanks.
- **Day-in-the-life**—Students write or draw imagined events in the daily life of an organism living in the place.
- **"I am like" poem**—Students choose an object, then write a sentence, "I am like [my object] because…" Repeat for several objects.
- **Differences from home**—Students write differences between this place and their home.

Meditative/reflective

- **Silence**—Students select a site they like, then sit alone without talking/signing for ten minutes. When they come back, ask them to share something they noticed or thought of in that place.
- **Relationship reflection**—As noted earlier, but students reflect on what value the place has, to whom, who is allowed to use it, and who is in charge. Share reflections in pairs afterwards.
- **Mental map**—Students draw a map of the place, illustrating features that are important to them and, after sharing, reflect on how their values led them to select those features as important (Valle, 2021).

Examples

Figure 5.6 Describing a scene to a peer who is trying to draw it

Figure 5.7 Meeting a tree while blindfolded

Figure 5.8 Making ephemeral art from natural objects

Getting Started via Exploration and Team Building

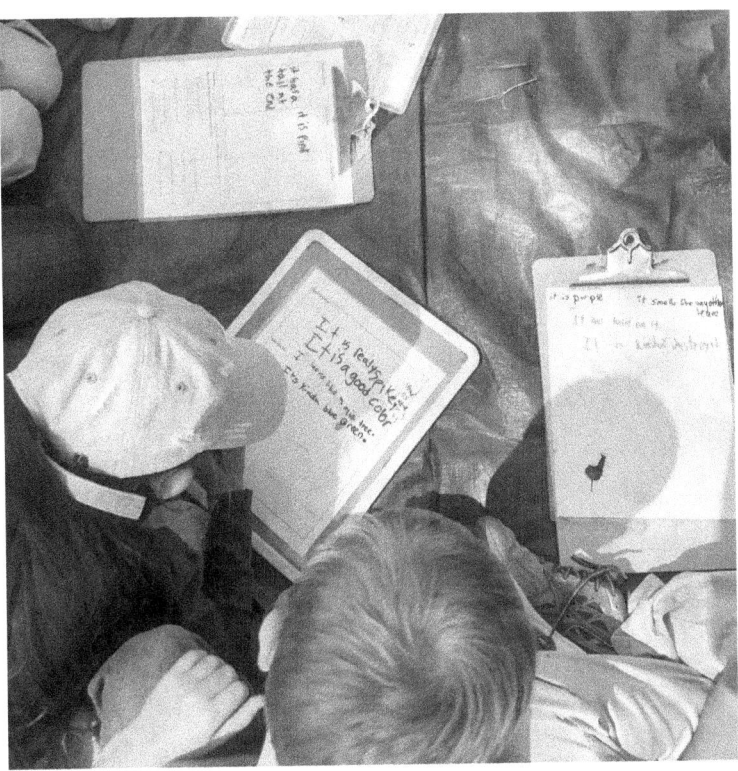

Figure 5.9 Circle observations of several objects

Figure 5.10 Writing natural history notes

Getting Started via Exploration and Team Building

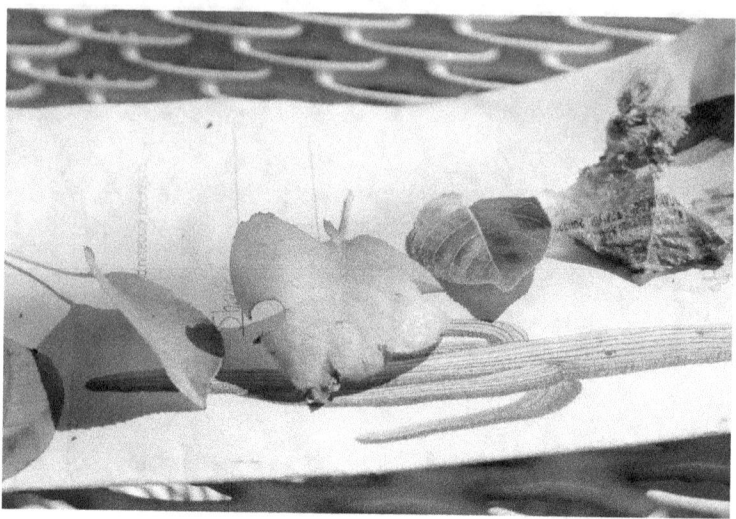

Figure 5.11 Gathering a color rainbow

Figure 5.12 Taking time for silence

5.4 Acquiring Background Information

Concepts

Background information helps students understand the value of a place and the relationships contained within it. It also helps your students understand what is already known about a place or about how key Disciplinary Core Ideas apply within it and can highlight ideas that others think are important. Prior knowledge from books or other sources can help students develop more sophisticated hypotheses (models) for the processes they might see or want to study.

However, too much background information can also hinder creativity and student ownership of the inquiry process by giving them the impression that everything is known about the topic already. To reduce this impression, you can keep the focus of the inquiry local—even if something is known about the question generally, student projects can uncover place-based answers.

Equity and Inclusion

Try not to overrepresent certain viewpoints or omit others (e.g., histories that begin with the arrival of white settlers). Your selection of sources implicitly teaches your students whose viewpoints are considered valuable. Even if you are consulting sources to gain factual information (e.g., rock properties), you are implicitly indicating that such knowledge is more relevant than other information (e.g., who uses the rocks). It is especially important to gain background information on the history and relationships inherent to your place.

Implementation

You can guide the selection of information sources to influence student engagement and the breadth of information students will have access to. You can use typical classroom techniques (e.g., jigsaw discussions, think-pair-share) and typical sources (e.g., books, Wikipedia, trustworthy websites) for background information. You can also have students speak with community members or find recorded interviews to learn more about the relationships within a place. The most surprising insight from background research on any place-based question is usually how little is known. This search for background information can be an opportunity for students to realize that much of how the world works is not yet understood.

Students can write in their notebooks to synthesize background information, using the following prompts:

- What is known, and what is unknown, about this topic?
- What emotions do you feel after learning this information?
- What do you want to do next or find out next?
- How is this information relevant to this place? To you?

Grade-Level Differentiation

Elementary (3–5)

Focus on student-led exploration and hands-on inquiry. Students have less discipline to accept what others know and less patience to do reading before going outside. After the inquiry project is complete, sharing background information may help students with sense-making when their interest and confidence are high.

Middle (6–8)

Be deliberate in choosing to present background information and in directing students toward particular topics or questions.

High (9–12)

More in-depth background information can be used.

Examples

Local species: In a middle school ecology unit in Arizona, the school district provided a textbook reading on invasive species that focused on Lake Victoria in Africa where the Nile perch is believed to be responsible for the extinction or severe decline of cichlid fish species. Student engagement was low because the lesson was about another set of facts about a faraway place to temporarily

Getting Started via Exploration and Team Building

Figure 5.13 Gathering background information on photosynthesis from a book (fourth grade)

Figure 5.14 Learning bird names from a book (fifth grade)

remember and then to forget. The lesson was changed to focus on a local issue: an invasive grass species, buffelgrass, which can outcompete and (through fire) kill the native saguaro cactus. With this new example, engagement and enthusiasm were far higher. Students could connect to their local place and understand how this species would influence their neighborhoods.

5.5 Recognizing Relationships and Responsibility to Place

Concepts

All places have relationships to people and are thus not blank ahistorical spaces in which learning occurs, even if they are apparently "pristine." Recognizing there are such relationships is important in framing inquiry projects and developing systems thinking. Past and present use by humans may explain phenomena that interest students and influence their relationships to the place. For example, learning about Indigenous rights to land may be useful in deciding what questions can be respectfully asked, or learning about current pollution from nearby industries may allow students to ask questions about the health of community members.

Recognizing relationships can also develop students' engagement as community members. Explorations of relationships often make students more aware of power dynamics and injustice inherent to place. Additionally, in exploring their own relationships with a place, students may situate themselves as future leaders who can take on the obligation of care and reciprocity with land.

For many Indigenous peoples, humans are understood to have strong and reciprocal relationships with other organisms, and these organisms themselves are understood also to have relationships to place (Kimmerer, 2013). Recognizing these place relationships may make learning more relevant and accessible to Indigenous students.

Equity and Inclusion

Some students initially may feel excluded from exploration of relationships if they have not felt themselves included in places, for example, students whose families have unstable housing or students who have been explicitly and historically excluded from certain places due to land seizure, redlining, slavery, or other processes. Conversely, students whose families have had long connections to land may feel challenged or excluded if their perspective is not recognized, or if their understanding of place (and their right to be in that place) is challenged by a greater understanding of others' exclusion. The current legal owner of land is not always the rightful or original owner of the land. Using the classroom to critically challenge narratives of who has power over land is vital for justice (Bang et al., 2014).

You should provide a space in which students can broaden their perspectives, begin to ask critical questions, and feel supported in their exploration, wherever their starting point. Recognize that students may differ strongly on interpretations of their responsibility to place.

Implementation

Before working with students, you should do background research about relationships in the place so that you can guide your students ethically through the inquiry process. It is fine to be on a co-discovery journey with your students.

After providing background material to students or inviting community members to share their perspectives on the place, guide conversations by asking students to journal in their notebooks, responding to the following questions:

- What is this place's name? If its name is not an Indigenous one, what is its Indigenous name?
- Which groups of people are currently using, or have historically used, this place? What is/was each of their relationships/uses?
- Why have these relationships changed over time?
- What would be a just use of the place in the future? Who would be involved and what would they be doing?
- How does this information influence the questions you are curious about?
- What are some of the impacts to other people of your inquiry project?

Start conversations from a foundation of respect and ethics, and use facilitation techniques that allow all students to share their perspectives. Think/pair/share activities or written reflections can be helpful. Be prepared for conversations to touch on issues related to displacement of Indigenous peoples, slavery, homesteading, economic development, pollution, or gentrification, for example. There will not be easy answers to disagreements. You do not have to be an expert on these topics or take a particular viewpoint, but you do need to be ready to facilitate the respectful sharing of perspectives and help students think critically about how their identities and viewpoints may influence the inquiry projects they choose to do.

Inquiry projects that focus purely on natural science questions (e.g., rock properties) should not omit this process, as carrying out the science without discussion of these topics implicitly teaches students that these topics are unimportant when learning about the world. At a minimum, discussions should consider the last two bullet points noted earlier.

Grade-Level Differentiation

Middle (6–8)

Students can research and share a land acknowledgment to formalize their knowledge of place relationships and their positionality. An acknowledgment typically focuses on recognizing Indigenous rights-holders to land and can also include more information on other relationships (e.g., settlement, urban development). Land acknowledgments should not be used as a "move to innocence" (Tuck & Yang, 2012) that justifies current power dynamics, but rather should be a starting point for justice-focused engagement with place. That is, a land acknowledgment is an artifact of a larger learning process and is insufficient as the process itself.

High (9–12)

As noted earlier.

Getting Started via Exploration and Team Building

Examples

Figure 5.15 Indigenous students visiting salmon traps managed by Nez Perce Tribe fisheries staff

Figure 5.16 Place use can be destructive or disrespectful; here, via riverbank erosion

Getting Started via Exploration and Team Building

Figure 5.17 Labeling a sample's location with its Tohono O'odham name (Babad Do'ag, Frog Mountain)

Trash mitigation: Students in a fourth-grade group observed a lot of trash in their schoolyard and identified that it was an ongoing problem. While they were not necessarily excited to pick up trash, they were empowered to make a change, and it quickly became a game to see who could collect the most trash.

Since the group was interested in where the trash was coming from, their strategy was to clean each of their target areas, then document the amount and types of trash they gathered, then do the same thing the next day to see where new trash was appearing. With this information, they made recommendations to school officials and to peers to try to reduce the amount of litter in their schoolyard.

The students were able to take on this project as a way to not only utilize scientific processes to analyze a problem but also to use what they learned to make a change. Some of the top school district administrators were in attendance for the students' final presentations. One of them expressed embarrassment over the schoolyard not being clean. By the end, the administrator got to see what a valuable learning opportunity it was for the students and how empowered they were to make a change. It is important when students take on projects that involve the opportunity

Getting Started via Exploration and Team Building

Figure 5.18 Collecting trash

for social change that they receive support to enact that change. In this case, students made recommendations on where to place garbage cans and informed the cafeteria staff what types of food products were creating the most garbage that was not being recycled or disposed of properly in the hope that changes could be made to cleaner or more sustainable options.

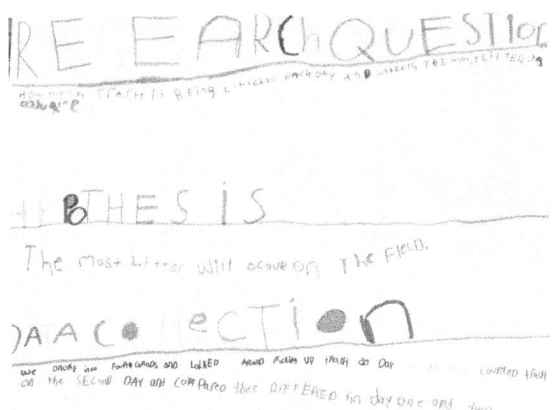

Figure 5.19 Inquiring about where trash originates

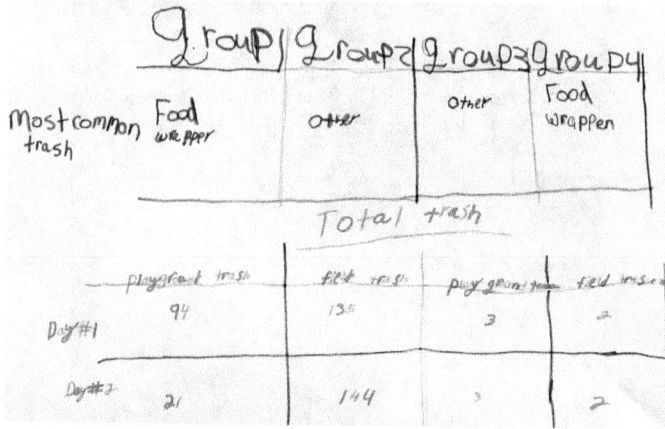

Figure 5.20 Finding that trash is more common on the playground one day and on the field another day

Figure 5.21 Graphs of trash counts and types

Facilitating Teams and Resolving Conflict

6.1 Small-Group Facilitation

Concepts

Because you are no longer providing direct instruction from the front of the classroom, students need your support with peer interactions and maintaining focus in small groups. Because students are no longer indoors, they need support to help them feel comfortable in a novel environment and to promote positive behaviors. Because students are leading their own projects, they need your guidance rather than your answers. In short, you should become a facilitator and lead from the back of the classroom.

Facilitated, student-centered teaching can look unproductive at first. Be prepared for an adjustment period if you are accustomed to close control over your classroom. However, it ultimately can reduce your stress and help students deepen their learning. It requires paying extra attention to group dynamics and student engagement and taking actions to guide those in productive directions.

Equity and Inclusion

Moving away from a teacher-centered classroom shifts power dynamics toward students. In doing so it empowers students to bring their own knowledge, thought processes, and capacities, promoting their inclusion. It also

DOI: 10.4324/9781003367192-6

This chapter has been made available under a CC-BY license.

amplifies broader issues of identity and power and marginalization within student groups. Small-group work can instead potentially yield less equitable outcomes than whole-classroom instruction.

To facilitate inclusively, you should provide students space to interact in ways where they feel powerful (i.e., without fear of authority or dominant perspectives from society or the curriculum). Avoid correcting terminology, grammar, or syntax as they discuss their ideas. If a student has an idea that seems surprising or wrong to you or other students, ask, "Why do you think that?" or "Why do you think they might think that?" rather than immediately giving an opinion of your own. You should also be conscious of power dynamics among students. Work with students to establish a set of norms for how they can confidently interact with each other.

A facilitative question-based approach can help students develop self-awareness of group dynamics and equity issues. If they make an insensitive comment or a joke about a stereotype, ask them to consider what their words say about the person targeted and how they imagine it might feel to have someone say those words about them. Be careful in questioning *not* to give the impression that discriminatory actions are equally valid options. If conflict arises, use restorative justice practices (Van Ness & Strong, 2014) to address any harm done, make amends, and reintroduce students back into the space.

Implementation

Clearly communicate the student-focused nature of the work to ensure students know that they are expected to succeed through their own initiative and teamwork. Set specific behavior-based ground rules and expectations for group work to help model teamwork for students and to provide clear expectations for what successful and unsuccessful group work looks like. Some suggested expectations include:

- Active listening
- Participation from all group members
- Positively framed communication and provisioning of critical feedback
- Commitment to team safety (e.g., sharing weight of equipment/water when walking, checking in on each other regularly)

Keep groups spatially separated to avoid distractions—if possible, have groups work in different areas so that they are better able to focus on their projects.

Defining roles can help a group recognize multiple types of contributions. You can assign roles to students in advance (e.g., recorder, measurer, equipment manager, artist) and also rotate students through roles at regular intervals. Alternatively, you can have students define and select roles themselves. Recognize that some students may want or need alternative ways to contribute (e.g., by making illustrations for group presentations or providing motivational support to the entire group).

Take time for sense of place or team building activities both early on and throughout a project, because they help support building student groups into effective teams. Do not be afraid to invest time in redirecting groups away from project work toward these activities.

Establish regular check-in points in advance (see the template in Appendix 1). You can have groups regularly check in with the entire class or with yourself about their progress. These check-ins can be good opportunities for students to take stock of their progress, synthesize their work, and evaluate their progress relative to their peers. It will also help you ensure students are accountable and making regular progress.

Do not provide answers to students' questions immediately (except questions of logistics/safety) or stop students from going down a path that appears to be wrong (except if it will clearly cause chaos or distress). You can instead provide limited facts or help students learn a skill and ask open-ended questions to guide their decision-making (see later). You can provide answers after students have tried to solve a problem themselves or if they are obviously stuck (Chapter 6). Much of students' learning will come as they work through questions by themselves.

Communicate respect for your students by not providing directive feedback except when related to logistics/safety and by normalizing failure and improvement. Allow students to move through a learning process that includes failure and abandonment of unsuccessful ideas. For example, you should feel more comfortable saying, "I need you to finish by lunchtime" or "That was a good idea, what will you try next?" than "Your idea was wrong." Your questions should engage all students in the group and should not single out particular students.

Other strategies for leveraging the power of open-ended questions include:

- **Asking general questions**—Can you tell me what you are doing (or thinking)? What would you do next? Why do you think you might be stuck? Why is this hard?

- **Asking questions that do not have yes/no answers**—What does X cause?

- **Answering questions with more questions**—If X were true, then why do you think you observed Y? How does doing Z help you find the answer to Y?

- **Asking probing questions to allow students to redirect their own thinking**—Have you noticed that X? What if you tried Y instead? What evidence makes you think Z is the right choice?

- **Asking process questions to help students identify their own questions**—What could you do to answer your question about X?

- **Asking more specific time-centered questions that leave the students in command**—Are you on track to finish X on time? What do you need to succeed?

- **Valuing student suggestions regardless of apparent factual correctness**—That is an interesting idea; why do you think that? (Regardless of whether you think a student is right or wrong, ask a question that allows them to deduce for themselves through further questioning whether their logic holds. Often the student's explanation shows you they are on the right track, or it may help you understand where their misconceptions have come from.)

- **Soliciting multiple answers**—What are the other ideas or opinions in the group?

- **Providing longer wait times for students as they think through questions**—We will wait 30 seconds for everyone to think. I will wait until I see three hands raised before we discuss.

- **Allowing students to discuss in pairs or teams before providing answers**—Share your thoughts with the person next to you, and then I will ask for your pair to share.

Facilitating Teams and Resolving Conflict

Examples

Figure 6.1 Facilitating in circles minimizes power hierarchies among students and the teacher (third from left)

Figure 6.2 A teacher (second from left) checks in on a student team

Facilitating Teams and Resolving Conflict

Figure 6.3 Students explain their project planning steps to a teacher (in baseball cap). Body positioning conveys support

6.2 Setting Behavioral Expectations

Concepts

Changing the location of teaching can drive changes in students' relationships, behaviors, and expectations. Behavior expectations are often one of two types:

- **Rules**—Decided on by people of authority
- **Norms**—Group-specific expectations that are reached by habit

Taking a class outside and asking students to conform to the same behavior rules and norms as in the classroom can be jarring for students and create unnecessary management problems for you. It is better to set clear expectations in the form of rules prior to going outside and make explicit any norms you want to establish from the very beginning of time outside.

Equity and Inclusion

Students will assume unspoken norms about behavior (e.g., toward plants and animals or other people). When these unspoken norms are violated, unnecessary conflict can occur. This can be especially stressful for students outside the dominant group. Discussing and explicitly stating unspoken norms can avoid this issue. It also can increase comfort levels for students who are not in a dominant group and may be unsure how they are expected to behave or who are uncomfortable with how others are behaving.

Implementation

You can set rules, especially around safety, as you deem necessary. However, collaborating on establishing norms is important for student buy-in. This process allows students to feel included in the decision-making process and part of the community. Circles are useful for these discussions, as they minimize unspoken power hierarchies. When establishing norms in a circle, provide time for students to brainstorm, and choose a sharing strategy that allows each student to speak (or write) their idea. As a class you can commit to all the norms or vote on a short list.

Acknowledge that outside is very different from an indoor classroom. Several areas to consider include:

- **Safety**—Discussed in Chapter 4.
- **Curiosity and exploration**—Underscore that students should expect a different context than in their classrooms, in that students will be expected to explore and guide their work along with their own interests and that there will no longer be any "right" questions or "right" answers.

- **Respect for place**—Explain the importance of caring for places that are homes to people and organisms (Chapter 5). Frame this conversation first in terms of moral responsibility and then secondarily in terms of particular proscriptive actions so that students feel an ability to self-govern the boundaries of appropriate behavior. You can collaboratively establish a set of proscriptive rules in conversations with your students. There will be a tension between respecting Leave No Trace (1987) principles and doing science (e.g., you may need to dig a hole to find worms). You may want to discuss:
    - If you move an object, should you put it back where you found it?
    - Can you walk anywhere you want?
    - What should you do with wrappers or food scraps from your lunch?

Places of high cultural significance may require setting additional expectations.

- **Respect for organisms**—Emphasize that students should not harm organisms through their projects (e.g., through unnecessary picking, capturing, harassing, or killing). Key questions to consider include:
    - Why might you feel grossed out by a certain organism?
    - How might your presence and interaction affect the behavior of the organism?
    - Could some organisms hurt you if they feel threatened?
    - What might be the consequences of feeding your food to animals?
    - Can touching or capturing an organism potentially spread disease to it or cause it stress?
    - Why does our behavior differ when interacting with organisms we encounter as pets? On a farm? When hunting/fishing/gathering?
- **Respect for others**—Make it clear that students are working on a team together and therefore are relying on each other for a constructive and safe learning environment by:
    - *Allowing all voices to be heard*—Emphasize that each person in the group needs to contribute for the group to be successful.

You can set specific rules, like requiring all students to provide an opinion before the group makes a decision about a question.
- *Taking care of one another's needs*—Emphasize that group members may have different needs but that all these needs should be met for the group to succeed. You can talk about the importance of taking breaks, of checking to see if other students are struggling and then helping them (e.g., by carrying something heavy, offering them a snack), etc.
- *Acknowledging different skills*—Emphasize that group members may contribute to the group's success in different ways. Some may be good at writing, others at measuring, and others at organizing; some may be adept artists who can visually represent the project in an effective way, etc.. Make sure students recognize that their peers can succeed in multiple ways.

- **Time and schedule**—With longer inquiry projects, students can lose track of time or lose confidence if they do not know when they will have their needs met (e.g., for bathrooms, lunch, or going home). Tell students what they can expect to occur at what time—and then follow through.

Grade-Level Differentiation

Elementary (3–5)

Some students will have little experience outside, so you should focus on developing norms. Be patient and consistent until norms have been established.

Middle (6–8)

Students may have more unspoken norms. Take time to discuss them and why students may have different norms.

High (9–12)

As noted earlier.

Facilitating Teams and Resolving Conflict

Examples

Figure 6.4 Students are empowered to climb a tree. The teacher has set a boundary for the maximum height students can climb

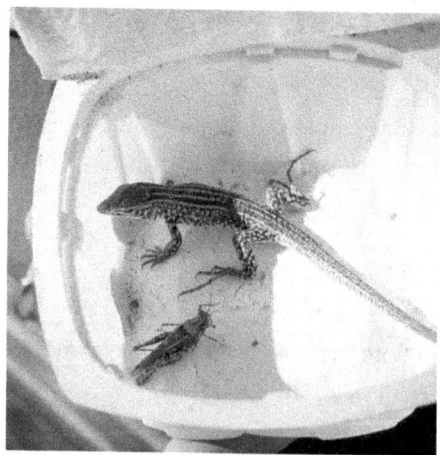

Figure 6.5 A lizard and cricket collected in a cereal container. Collection followed a discussion of respectful animal handling

Facilitating Teams and Resolving Conflict

Figure 6.6 Tree bark is disrespectfully carved with names

6.3 Encouraging Positive Behavior from Individuals

Concepts

Students will behave differently without the normal routine and hierarchy of a classroom environment—and not always in ways you might expect. Some will be excited to be outside; others, scared; some will see an opportunity to escape discipline or socialize with friends; others will want to explore alone; some will stay close, and others will want to wander. Common sets of positive and negative behaviors can thus emerge. Because being outside is higher-risk than the classroom and is potentially more likely to make students uncomfortable, outside-specific approaches should be used to address these behaviors.

Equity and Inclusion

Leaving the classroom provides a novel context for students to assert their power over each other. Be mindful of potential discrimination occurring as certain behaviors emerge (e.g., if students in majority identities disproportionately exhibit certain behaviors).

Implementation

Some student behaviors are constructive and can be reinforced. These include students who:

- **Improve behavior**—A student who is reticent or behaviorally challenging in a classroom, but who opens up or engages strongly when given a new context. *What to do:* Recognize positive changes and reinforce engagement.
- **Use tools**—A student who becomes extremely engaged by using new tools. *What to do:* Be sure tools are used safely for their intended purpose, and encourage them to think how they can use them to advance their project. Encourage the student to share their knowledge and engage in other aspects of the project.
- **Make observations**—A student who notices many natural phenomena (e.g., insects that other students do not see, or distinguishes between different kinds of plants, or a student who enjoys journaling, drawing, or taking photographs of what they observe). *What to do:* Encourage students to share observations with others.
- **Explore the environment**—A student who enjoys exploring a place on their own or who is more comfortable in novel outdoor settings. *What to do:* Encourage enthusiasm.
- **Solve problems**—A student who thinks of creative solutions for problems the group is facing. *What to do:* Give positive feedback and assist the student in sharing and/or implementing their ideas with the group.
- **Help the group**—A student who cooperates, asks for clarification, checks on group dynamics, or inspires or motivates others (Pfund et al., 2012). *What to do:* Give positive feedback.

Facilitating Teams and Resolving Conflict

Other student behaviors can be less constructive in the context of a focused inquiry group process. Here are some common patterns and ideas for redirection. Some behaviors arise from students having limited impulse control or experiencing larger challenges. Many behaviors arise from students working outside of their comfort zone (e.g., outside, with peers). You may not be able to redirect all behaviors within the scope of an inquiry project. Students also may shift between behaviors. Students may:

- **Dominate/direct others**—A student who takes a directive role, possibly (though not necessarily) to help lead the group, who blocks or rushes others, or who discounts others' opinion (Pfund et al., 2012). *What to do:* Create systems for all students to provide input (e.g., Each student gets three Popsicle sticks to use, one for each idea shared. The Popsicle sticks get replenished once every student has used all of theirs). Suggest that students swap roles in the group; gently suggest that another student learn/take over the role; take the student aside and ask them privately to change their behavior; or give the student a specific role that involves more individual tasks and less group dynamics (e.g., measuring a certain thing repeatedly).
- **Overshare opinions/facts**—A student who has many facts to share, opinions on the right way to do things, or apparently more experience in a place than others. *What to do:* If possible, give the student a task that they are unfamiliar with (outdoor exploration or measuring rather than asking questions or generating hypotheses); or ask them to make space for their peers' learning and ideas. A more equal system for sharing can also be utilized like in the previous example.
- **Disengage from the group**—A student who does not appear to be paying attention to the group or is distracted by some item in the place (e.g., digging a hole). *What to do:* Consider redirecting the group to focus productively on the same item as this student; give the student a role requiring more active attention; pair the student with another more engaged student on a common task; or pause to have the group summarize its progress and goals in case the student has lost the thread of the work.
- **Wander**—A student who does not stay with the group and is off exploring the place and/or not contributing to group work.

What to do: Give the student a task that allows them to explore (e.g., scouting research locations, finding organisms; give the student a role requiring more active attention; or pair the student with another more engaged student on a common task, or ask them to be your assistant for some time).

- **Destroy things**—A student who is more interested in modifying than observing their environment (e.g., breaks branches, throws rocks) or a student who is actively destructive (e.g., kills insects, uproots plants). *What to do:* Communicate immediately that the behavior is unacceptable for reasons of respect for the place and the people/organisms who use it; through discussion and reflection, set boundaries for acceptable behavior; if the behavior is enthusiastic rather than mean-spirited, try to redirect into productive exploration/measurement actions (possibly with demonstrations); or pair the student with another and ask them to complete a task together.

- **Withdraw**—A student who does not interact much with other students in the group or who does not volunteer answers when asked. *What to do:* Check for any unmet needs (see "Feel uncomfortable" later); pause to have the group summarize its progress and goals in case the student has lost the thread of the work; ask the student if there is a role they would like to try out; pair the student with another and ask them to complete a task together; or find a task that is compatible with quiet work and engagement (e.g., recording data, scouting sites).

- **Feel afraid or express prejudices**—A student who thinks the place or the people in it are dirty, inhuman, or scary. *What to do:* This may be the student's first time in such a place if their home life is very different. This experience can be a learning opportunity, but it is also important not to overwhelm an anxious student. Assure the student of their safety (e.g., from animal attacks or crime); if possible, allow them to slowly become comfortable around whatever is causing distress (possible initially by allowing more distance). Take the student aside privately to have a conversation about respect if needed; otherwise, use questioning to promote reflection about their discomfort. Consider further teaching/discussion around the underlying social issues if relevant.

- **Feel alienated**—A student who does not feel they belong in the place or who feels angry/uncomfortable/sad that the place is nicer than their home neighborhood. *What to do:* As noted earlier in "Feels afraid".
- **Feel uncomfortable**—A student who is obviously physically or emotionally uncomfortable or who is quiet in worrying ways. *What to do:* Take the student aside and determine whether they have any unmet physical needs (e.g., get warm, use a toilet, eat a snack, rest, see a nurse) or emotional needs (e.g., recent conflict with other group members, anxiety around being outside, bad associations with the place), then address the need directly in private or with the entire group (e.g., suggest everyone take a snack break together). Sometimes a student will be concerned about something outside of school, and you may not be able to offer a solution; nonetheless, you should establish a norm of care.

Redirection can occur by re-establishing goals, or by privately asking students if their behavior is consistent with what they agreed to in their team contract, or the norms you set at the beginning of the project. Additional strategies include:

- **Task-setting**—Find a specific task for a participant to carry out (e.g., measure X, carry Y, take photos of Z). Having a recognized and needed role may help unengaged participants re-engage.
- **Redirecting attention**—Use an interesting natural history observation or game break to disrupt or divert problem behavior while also giving participants positive attention.
- **Forecasting**—Use statements like, "We have two more measurements to take, then we will take a lunch break" to empower students to plan and focus on the task at hand. This can also be used to prevent or stop whining.
- **Timing activity chunks**—Similar to forecasting, give the student increments for how long they will need to attend before a task is switched or they are offered a break.
- **Proximity**—Use your physical proximity to silently indicate to a student their behavior needs to change (e.g., talking while they should be listening).

- **Signaling**—Set up a secret signal with a participant who has a recurring behavior issue or concern, especially a behavior they are unaware of. This can help the student self-correct their behavior without unwanted group attention.
- **Praise**—Praise helpful behavior to help set expectations and encourage positive group dynamics (e.g., "Thanks for picking up that trash on the ground").
- **Removal**—As a last option, remove, or suggest the possibility of removing, a student from the group for a temporary cooling-off period.

Examples

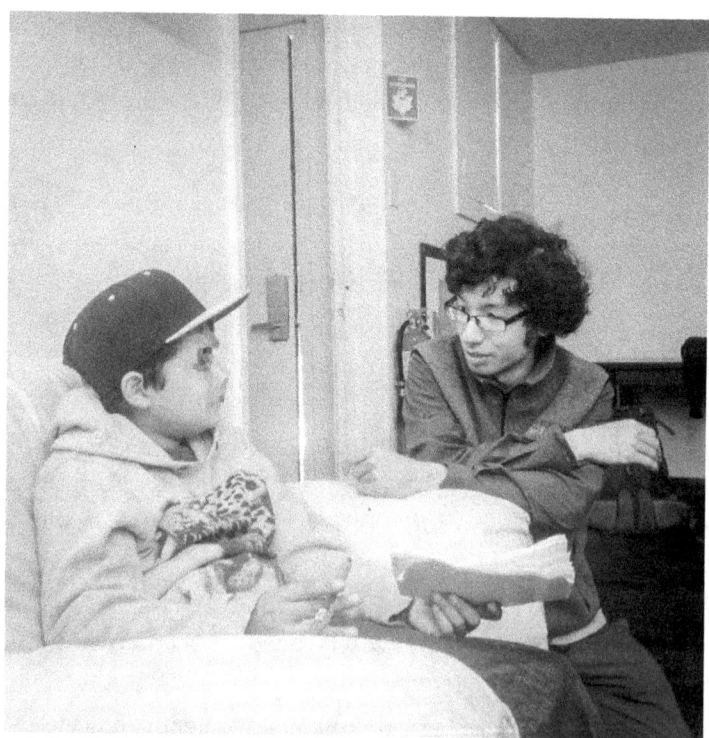

Figure 6.7 Sitting down for a one-on-one conversation

Facilitating Teams and Resolving Conflict

Figure 6.8 A student who drew beavers climbing tree-stump skyscrapers and flying military airplanes during observation time was redirected to drawing animal illustrations for their team's presentation

6.4 Encouraging Positive Behavior from Groups

Concepts

Positive student behavior is the difference between a project that is frustrating and discouraging and one that is empowering and productive. Encouraging positive behavior requires active consideration of both individual actions and group processes. Positive behavior may not occur without active facilitation, especially when working with students who have little trust of each other or you at the beginning of an inquiry project.

Student behavior in groups changes through several stages over the course of a project. A widely used framework for group development includes five stages (Tuckman, 1965). *Forming* groups are coming together and trust is not yet in place; *storming* groups have begun to face challenges but relationships among members are not yet established, leading to necessary and productive conflict; *norming* groups are then resolving conflict and building trust; *performing* groups are achieving shared goals due to these issues being resolved; and *adjourning* groups are facing more conflict or less engagement as members begin to invest less in their group identity.

Groups typically move forward through these stages but can stagnate or move backwards when setbacks occur. Be mindful of where your groups are within these stages in order to anticipate what students may need at different points.

Equity and Inclusion

Conflict is a necessary component of group development. However, many students are not accustomed to moving through conflict in healthy and respectful ways. Student identities and life experiences can exacerbate differences in conflict resolution strategies and interpretations of others' behavior. Students' behaviors in groups cannot be decoupled from their home life patterns and conflicts, some of which may be traumatic and not yet well-processed. White supremacy culture particularly discourages conflict in favor of an absolute viewpoint in which certain powerful people are always correct (Jones & Okun, 2001). You should normalize conflict and provide tools for students to communicate effectively and recognize the identity-based barriers they may need to overcome toward this goal. You should also accept that larger conflicts students experience at home may constrain the progress they are able to make in school. If a school counselor is available, you may want to invite them to join the project for a day to provide further guidance.

When groups do experience conflict, assess whether certain students are held responsible based on their identities. Student identities may result in real and valuable differences in their conflict approaches, but also may cause some students to become the target of conflict due to discrimination. Consider using questioning strategies (as noted earlier) or restorative justice practices (Van Ness & Strong, 2014) to address these points as early as possible.

Implementation

Build a foundation of trust via team building. Team building is an investment in group dynamics. Do not hesitate to redirect groups from inquiry to team building if they are not progressing through stages.

When a group is forming, you should expect more of the group to be quiet, as students increase their comfort level with their peers and find their particular roles. You may also see groups that appear unfocused but are in the process of necessary exploration of each other or their inquiry question. You may not want to intervene where individual students do not seem to be engaged, as they may still be finding their place. You can consider giving feedback around the feasibility of the project, its implications for engaging all students, or providing key facts or ways to find facts that will shape student thinking.

When a group is storming or norming, you should expect more participation and more conflict or disagreement. You may want to intervene to promote healthy interpersonal interactions (e.g., remind students of their team contract) or to offer additional tools for speaking and listening. You can consider giving feedback around the progress the group is making toward becoming a team or suggesting issues that the group should consider related to its dynamics or the inquiry. This is a key time to invest effort in actively facilitating the group.

When a group is performing, you should expect all students to be engaged and contributing productively. You can consider giving feedback around the appropriateness of methods or the correct use of equipment/data recording. You can spend less time actively facilitating the group.

When a group is adjourning, you should expect students to lose some engagement or focus. You should remind students of their shared purpose or take actions to improve engagement (e.g., team building activities or reflection).

Help students recognize that conflict will occur and is healthy and that respectful and low-stakes conflict is a key part of the inquiry learning process. Strategies to make conflict low-stakes include:

- Acknowledge conflict early, before action has already been taken and a group's project rides on the outcome of the conflict.

- Help groups decide how they will handle conflict in respectful discussions so that group members are not afraid to voice opinions by not knowing what the response will be.
- Encourage groups to seek explicit affirmative consensus, rather than a leader acting on consensus by silence (lack of verbal objections). This creates opportunities for speaking up with disagreements and for finding solutions.
- Model restorative justice practices that encourage students to identify ways to repair harm and talk through group needs instead of removing a member from the activity altogether.

These dynamics can be difficult to monitor simultaneously in multiple groups. You can bring multiple groups together for whole-class check-ins to assess dynamics. Seeing peer progress or reflecting on their own group's progress can sometimes help student groups move between stages.

Students may be better able to recognize and self-regulate group dynamics if they are familiar with what to expect. Consider presenting Tuckman's stages of group development and leading a discussion of what actions each group can incorporate to recognize and act on those (e.g., team contracts during forming, reflection time during adjourning).

Grade-Level Differentiation

Elementary (3–5)

State the importance of care for self and care for others. Suggest explicit phrases for voicing an opinion about a group plan or activity and for resolving disagreement.

Middle (6–8)

Discuss the need for and benefit of conflict and disagreement. Model resolution strategies and emphasize that disagreement does not need to be taken personally.

High (9–12)

As noted earlier. Discuss group development stages and strategies for dealing with conflict at each stage.

Facilitating Teams and Resolving Conflict

Examples

Figure 6.9 Working together to place a measuring tape over rocks for a vegetation transect

Figure 6.10 Snacks shared among the team provide an opportunity to relax and re-energize

Facilitating Teams and Resolving Conflict

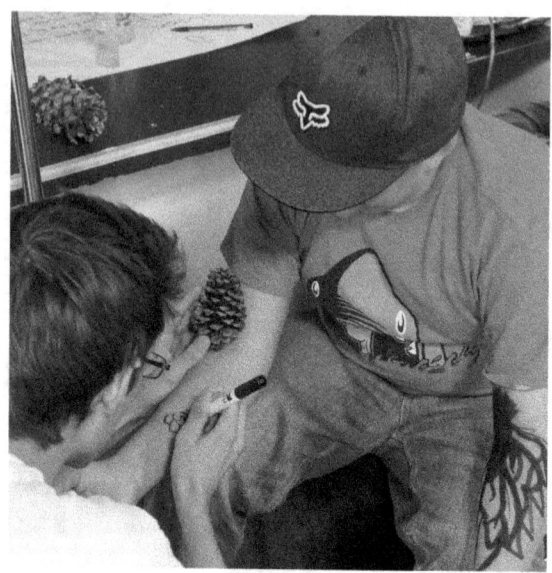

Figure 6.11 Building team identity through shared experience; here, giving permanent marker plant tattoos

Figure 6.12 Marking shared team identity through art; here, a cartoon of a teacher (left), a volunteer (second from left), and student team members

6.5 Team Building

Concepts

When students are assigned into a group, they are not yet a team. They may not have any shared experience or trust, or even know each other. Teamwork requires interpersonal relationships to be negotiated. To build a group into a team, they need to establish trust and shared experience and develop approaches for acknowledging and resolving conflicts. Team building activities model this process. While these activities may not always appear to be directly linked to inquiry projects you are facilitating, they provide a foundation. They also help students learn how their peers behave in challenging situations.

Learning outcomes from team building include building positive collaboration, communication, and listening skills. For example, developing respectful communication and active listening skills will help students develop project ideas and interpret results; sharing responsibilities through a challenge will help students divide responsibilities and collaborate during an inquiry project. These skills also can transfer to the student's classroom learning or personal development.

Team building activities can be fun challenges or games for students. Spending time on these activities can provide physical and mental breaks for students, help maintain engagement, and delineate milestones during the day.

Equity and Inclusion

Team building can intensify the power dynamics that students experience daily. Invest time in reflection to build positive interactions, and step in early to cut off inappropriate behavior when needed. Chapter 13 provides facilitation strategies.

Implementation

Begin with team building, rather than with inquiry. If you rush into the inquiry process right away, your students may not yet be prepared to work well with each other or to think about their local place (their schoolyard or park) critically. By taking time to develop these areas, you will have more success later.

Introduce activities to the whole class, then implement with multiple small teams in parallel. You may want to allow students to repeat the activity (to improve performance) after they discuss outcomes within teams. After one or a few repetitions, hold a reflection session.

Reflection allows students to scaffold their experience into principles and trust they can apply within their inquiry projects. Reflection should mirror the teamwork and conflict resolution processes used in projects. Ask students to use "I. . . " or "When you do X. . . I feel. . . Y" statements when talking. Ensure only one person speaks at a time and that all students have a chance to speak at least once (e.g., by passing around a ball or stick that grants the holder speaking privileges). Gathering in a circle helps signal equality.

Example questions to ask students:

- Was this activity hard? Why?
- What is one thing that went well or poorly in the activity?
- Who was a leader? Who was a follower? Who wanted a different role?
- What is one thing another person did that helped everyone succeed?
- Why did we do this activity?

Time spent on team building activities should be considered an investment in enabling future success. You may be tempted to skip these activities, thinking that your students already know each other and work together well. Team building helps prime inquiry groups for immediate success and also helps set behavioral expectations as students work together in teams that may bring together students who usually do not spend time with each other. Each activity may take 10–20 minutes and may save one to two hours of lost student time later on. For a week-long project you may consider interspersing three to four activities within the project.

All activities should be done in small groups. Additional activities can be found in Bordessa (2005) and Price et al. (2015). All activities can be made more challenging by restricting students' methods of communicating (e.g., no talking, no signing) or by providing a time limit.

Getting to know names and each other

- **Introduce your partner (paired activity)**—Have students interview each other in pairs according to a set of questions you prepare. Have them then "introduce" the students to the rest of the team.
- **Five things in common**—Ask students to talk and find five items that all members of their team share in common. Have groups compare their list to other groups and give points to teams that have unique items.

- **Animal noises**—Put one student in the center of a circle of the other students. The center student closes their eyes and spins around, then stops after a few seconds. They then point at the person in front of them. The center student names an animal (e.g., goose) and the student being pointed at has to make that animal's noise. If the center student can guess the name of the student on the outside of the circle, they switch; otherwise, repeat, or switch after two to three incorrect guesses.

Building communication skills

- **Human knot**—All students make a circle and put their hands in the middle, joining each hand with a different person. The challenge is then to unknot the group without releasing hands. The final possible outcomes are (1) one large circle, (2) two smaller disjunct circles, or (3) two smaller circles chained to each other; all are successes.
- **Blindfolded search**—Choose one student to blindfold. Place an object somewhere on the ground away from the blindfolded student. The blindfolded student's task is to find the object. The rest of the team is allowed to talk to the student to give them instructions but cannot move themselves.
- **Rope shape-making**—Have a loop of rope, about one meter of rope per student. Give it to the students, each holding part of it. Have them all close their eyes. Challenge them as a group to make a geometric shape (e.g., equilateral triangle). They are not allowed to open their eyes or take both hands off the rope, but can move.
- **Magic stick**—Get a meter stick or a long plant branch. It should be lightweight. Introduce the stick as magical because it will fly up to the sky if no one is holding on to it. Challenge the students to lower it to the ground. While holding the stick, have all students put a single finger under the stick somewhere along its length. They are not allowed to let go of the stick or touch the top of the stick (if they do, the game restarts). The stick will likely start rising or moving due to pressure imbalances from fingers. Students win when the stick is flat on the ground.
- **Lava river**—Get several square foam pads or bits of tarp. Define a distance (maybe five meters) that is a river full of lava the students have to cross. The pads are lava-proof, so students with a foot on one can use them to cross the river. Once a pad is on the river, it cannot move

until it is picked up again. If there is ever a pad with no one touching it, then it is lost. If any student falls in, the team starts over. Begin with five to six pads for a group of eight students. As a "lava monster," steal pads from students to make the game harder.

- **Lava lake**—Find a large rock or sidewalk block. Tell students that lava is filling their site, and they will catch fire unless they can all stand on the platform above the lava. They have to be able to balance without falling on the platform for at least ten seconds. Once they succeed, tell them that the lava is rising and the platform is getting smaller. Find a smaller object and repeat.

Building positive relationships

- **Predator-prey**—One person is a predator in the center of an area, standing over a pile of resources (sticks/water bottles). All other students are prey trying to get some of the resources in the center. First, all prey scatter and hide. In a round, the predator closes their eyes and counts down from ten. At zero, they can look around but not move. If they see any prey, they can try to identify them by name or description. Correct identification means that the prey is "out." Repeat until only one prey remains or all the resources are taken. You can add variants where prey can cooperate or where multiple types of resources can be collected.
- **Trust fall and pass-around**—Make a tight circle with one person in the middle. All students in the circle are in a brace position with hands up. The person in the middle closes their eyes and falls over, keeping their body rigid. As they fall, people on the side gently push them back to the center, and they "float" in the air. This activity requires the introduction of safe/acceptable ways to touch another person.
- **Laser eyes**—Students stand in a circle looking down. When you say, "look up" all students pick another student and look at their eyes. If two students mutually look at each other, the lasers in their eyes resonate and both students explode (have them make a noise); they are out of the game. Look down, then repeat for more rounds until either one or two students remain as a winner.
- **Monster game**—Students create a monster out of their bodies, which has a certain number of legs/arms/heads. Students then link bodies until they achieve the desired features. Ask students to show how their monster moves by having it move its limbs without it falling apart.

Grade-Level Differentiation

Elementary (3–5)

Be prepared for groups becoming frustrated or unable to understand how to solve a team building challenge. In these cases you may need to provide additional guidance or hints. See later.

Middle (6–8)

Set clear behavioral expectations for appropriate types of physical touch in activities that require it (e.g., only hands/shoulders, no causing pain), if school guidelines do not already exist.

High (9–12)

As noted earlier.

Examples

Figure 6.13 Magic stick

Facilitating Teams and Resolving Conflict

Figure 6.14 Lava river, with blue foam pads

Figure 6.15 Predator-prey, with predator in center

Facilitating Teams and Resolving Conflict

Figure 6.16 Monster game

6.6 Team Contracts and Check-Ins

Concepts

Working on a team is effective when a common set of values and a high level of trust exist. Team members should set expectations for what to expect from each other's behavior, how they will work together, what they want to achieve, how they will handle conflict, what skills each student brings, and how to get in touch (if working out of school). Preparing a team contract sets clear expectations and promotes healthy discussion in advance of conflicts. In the case that conflict does occur later, it provides a mechanism to promote conflict resolution and accountability.

Mid-project check-ins provide a time for students to provide feedback on how their projects are going. This enables them to recognize their teammates for helpful behaviors and also works toward conflict resolution for unhelpful behaviors. Setting a formal context for check-ins normalizes feedback and healthy conflict and ensures that there is at least one opportunity for improvement to occur.

Equity and Inclusion

Contracts and check-ins empower students who might not usually speak up or feel comfortable in group settings. These structures enable these students to have their voices heard and listened to. Because some students may be less comfortable expressing their needs, it can be helpful for students to write down their needs privately or anonymously before sharing with peers.

Students may begin with limited empathy for the needs of their teammates if those needs differ strongly from theirs. Consider journaling exercises that allow students to share more information about themselves to help others understand their needs.

A contract and check-in are only helpful if students are accountable to what has been agreed upon. Take the conflict resolution process seriously. Otherwise, you may inadvertently teach students who may already be in marginalized positions that their needs are subordinate to those of other students.

Implementation

Introduce the team contract and check-in expectations during the inquiry project process so that expectations are clear. Start the team contract after students have met each other and gotten to know each other through initial team building or sense-of-place activities, so that some baseline trust is in place. Begin from a template document (see Appendix 1) and have students create a consensus document. Give students a copy for their own reference and keep a copy for yourself.

Start the check-in midway through the project (see the template in Appendix 1). Gather students and ask them to revisit their team contract and reflect on their behaviors. Ask them to share feedback on what they (as a team) should start, stop, or continue doing.

In cases of conflict or low performance, use the team contract as a starting point for encouraging student accountability via group discussions. You should acknowledge in a group setting that conflict is occurring, but should resolve the conflict privately to maintain respect for affected students. Ask for critical feedback about individuals to be shared with you privately instead of in groups. Use facilitation techniques (Chapter 13) to guide private discussions with students.

Grade-Level Differentiation

Elementary (3–5)

Minimize writing and instead gather consensus through a discussion about how students would like to be treated. Integrate any existing classroom standards for behaviors such as kindness and respect. Expect to personally check in frequently on appropriate behavior.

Middle (6–8)

Instead of using a template, have students write out their own expectations of their peers on a whiteboard, then discuss to generate a consensus set of items for the team.

High (9–12)

Each group can develop their own contract using a template. Have groups share their contracts with the whole class and discuss, then give groups more time to see if they want to modify their contract based on other ideas they liked.

Examples

Figure 6.17 Team contract (fourth grade) with signatures in the center

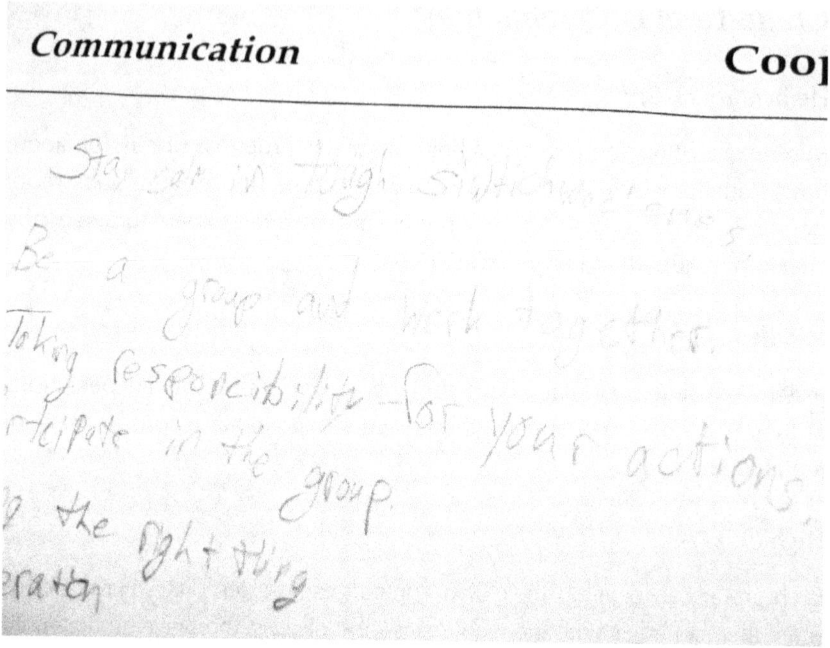

Facilitating Teams and Resolving Conflict

Communication   **Coo**

[handwritten notes, partially legible:]
Stay calm in tough situations
Be a group and work together.
Taking responsibility for your actions
[participate] in the group.
[Do] the right thing

Figure 6.18 Team contract (fifth grade)

Person	Skill contributions	Skill development areas
▆	My skills include organization and content knowledge, and working together to accentuate everyone in the group's strengths.	I have difficulty with time management and focusing.
▆	I am eager to take into account everyone's knowledge and experience, compromising on projects. I also communicate well on deadlines and ensure my participation.	I can be shy initially and have some issues with procrastination.
▆	My strongest skill sets include communication, creativity and compromise. Often when working in groups I try to include and promote all ideas brought to the table.	I have some difficulty speaking up about my own ideas, and have a tendency to speak a bit more informally than I should.

Figure 6.19 Digital team contract

6.7 Handling Multiple Groups

Concepts

When a class is divided into groups, you have to make choices about where to invest your attention. Student-centered teaching means that you will not need to monitor each individual as much as you may be used to, and letting go of some of that control is what allows students to learn responsibility and self-efficacy. Your task is to identify which groups may be derailed due to conflict or distraction or confusion. With small groups, you will be able to effectively facilitate while paying attention to each individual within the group, but at the price of having less time with each group.

Larger groups means fewer groups; however, larger groups are less functional due to unclear student roles, more likely off-task behavior, and a greater probability of conflict. Larger groups also mean your attention is more likely to be taken by few individuals and that students feel less responsibility and self-efficacy.

Equity and Inclusion

Be alert to your own tendencies to spend more time with certain groups. Some groups may need more support, while others may be more self-sufficient, but reflect regularly on which evidence or criteria you are using to allocate that time and how it relates to the identity of students in the groups. This reflection can be helpful for identifying your own patterns of behavior to see if you need to make any adjustments.

Implementation

Working with volunteers can help keep group size small, but even with volunteers you will need to balance between the needs of multiple groups. You can:

- **Float between groups**—You should regularly walk between groups to do short check-ins. Visit groups in random order so students do not know when to expect you. Check-ins also give you a chance to gauge progress and keep projects and behavior on track. Observe groups before making any conclusions or taking actions. You can also volunteer to help students by taking part in their work (e.g., by offering to record data).

- **Rely on other adults**—If possible, recruit other adults (Chapter 4) to help float between groups. In many cases, students will simply need an adult figure to keep them focused.
- **Set a timetable for the day's work**—You should set expectations for times at which students should reach sub-goals (e.g., deciding their methods) or should take breaks (e.g., for snacks or lunch). These smaller time goals can help keep groups on track by allowing them to reach smaller milestones. Give reminders before time is up to support transitions.
- **Have regular check-ins**—Set expectations that students will need to summarize their progress on different tasks to you or to peer groups in a whole-classroom context. You can also offer time for groups to come to you for a formal consultation or to ask questions if they get stuck on some aspect of their project.
- **Be comfortable with some chaos**—Having several small groups working independently outside will never look as controlled or organized as in a classroom. Changing your expectations can reduce your stress.

Grade-Level Differentiation

Elementary (3–5)

Supervision is critical in small groups, so volunteers are especially useful.

Middle (6–8)

Students may get sidetracked by social or environmental distractions. Focus on floating between groups for regular check-ins.

High (9–12)

Give students more independence in project management while communicating clear expectations for project progress. Provide more supervision initially and transition to a hands-off approach. Encourage groups to come to you with problems and questions, giving them space to work through issues on their own before deciding they need help.

Facilitating Teams and Resolving Conflict

Examples

Figure 6.20 Student groups working out of hearing distance but within the line of sight of adults

Figure 6.21 Keeping groups separated while walking minimizes distractions

6.8 Getting Groups Back on Track

Concepts

Sometimes a group can appear to be stuck and can remain in that state until you intervene. This is especially common with students who have not worked together before or with students who are not accustomed to the challenges of independent thinking or behavior management. Groups can also get stuck when they run into a major obstacle they are unable to solve, when they no longer understand what they are doing, or when they lose motivation. The latter three scenarios can occur in a cascading sequence, so it is important to provide help for stuck groups early on.

Ideally, students should find their own ways of getting unstuck, though you can facilitate. They are usually capable of resolving the obstacle, gaining understanding, or building intrinsic motivation. This can require patience, as you may be able to think of a solution from your own experience, but sharing that solution may increase a group's dependence on you and promote undesired power dynamics. Instead, you may need to let a group take an unfruitful path, experience conflict and setbacks, then provide questions and reflection to support them in moving past their challenge.

Equity and Inclusion

Providing low-stakes opportunities for initial failure and later success is empowering. Remind students regularly of their ownership of the process and of the learning goals associated with the process, rather than some outcome on paper, especially if they seem to be experiencing anxiety. Some students may not be as comfortable with low-stakes failure than others due to family resources and socialization.

Be careful to not assume your cultural expectations are being implicitly applied to student groups. For example, the volume of a discussion (very quiet or very loud) may not indicate a problem is occurring, depending on the students' identities.

Implementation

You can often notice a stuck group when students are clearly off-task, are not interacting with each other, appear uncomfortable (e.g., not making eye contact, doodling, playing with sticks), are experiencing negative interpersonal dynamics, or are unable to answer basic questions about the project and their progress.

A few strategies include:

- **Taking immediate action**—In cases involving potential physical or emotional harm, you should intervene immediately.
- **Acknowledging**—Validate students' experience of being stuck as natural and as an opportunity to learn strategies for moving past that stuck point.
- **Doing nothing**—Sometimes the best way to support a student's learning is to do nothing at all and to allow them to work through their thought process and mistakes independently. You should try to respect their learning process and resist micromanaging. Stay aware of their process in case you need to intervene.
- **Taking a break**—Concentrating for extended periods of time can be difficult. Running around, eating a snack, or exploring the place can help students come back to a project ready to succeed.
- **Having a conversation on group dynamics**—Determine what is working and what is not working. Sometimes you will need to intervene if some students' behavior is preventing others' success. Frame interventions as open-ended questions, and let students come to conclusions and make the decisions themselves whenever possible.
- **Summarizing**—Ask students to tell you what they know, what they do not know, what they want to know, and what they think they need help with. They can share either with you or with a partner.
- **Simplifying**—Ask students what they can change in their project to make it more interesting or more doable (e.g., reducing the number of variables measured or changing the question).

- **Sharing and reviewing**—Provide a few key pieces of information or ideas as hints to help the group move forward. You may temporarily need to pivot away from inquiry to direct instruction if there are key concepts students need to understand but do not yet (e.g., how to make a graph).

Avoid giving explicit directive feedback (e.g., "You need to measure X differently" or "Your idea is wrong"). Such feedback can be discouraging and detrimental to the group process. Students may sometimes learn more if they make a mistake or if their question's answer is unexpected or undesired.

You should give directive feedback primarily when it is oriented around group process or planning. For example, you can ask students to spend more time considering their hypotheses or to wrap up a certain measurement, or tell students they need to finalize their data analysis by a certain time.

Directive feedback is useful if you foresee students making choices that will prevent them from finishing their work on time or that will yield a study that is wrong with a failure mode that is uninteresting. For example, a group may spend most of their time planning their work or may fail to measure something because they are using their equipment incorrectly. While both situations still represent learning experiences, you can provide directive feedback early on to enable more useful learning experiences to occur.

Grade-Level Differentiation

Elementary (3–5)

Provide more direction on timelines and milestones.

Facilitating Teams and Resolving Conflict

Examples

Figure 6.22 Listening to a student explain a data analysis challenge

Figure 6.23 Sometimes taking a break is a good idea

Developing a Question and Study Design

7.1 Facilitating Question Development

Concepts

An inquiry project answers a specific question about the world. The question should be meaningful to students. Their connections to a place, societal values, prior or traditional knowledge, and curiosity can all influence their choices. Students should lead the question generation process with your facilitation and support.

The question's answer should be unknown. If an answer is already known, no inquiry needs to be made; similarly, if an unexpected answer will not be accepted, the process cannot uncover new knowledge. Letting the observations and data determine the answer develops confidence and connection to place through discovery.

Identifying a strong question requires creativity. It can be facilitated by focusing on an exploration stage, in which students gather ideas without prejudgment, often by allowing an environment to inspire them, and a winnowing stage, in which students take gathered ideas and evaluate them, with more structured criteria, to arrive at a final choice.

Equity and Inclusion

Students with identities that differ from yours may develop questions that you do not find as interesting or relevant. Hold your criticism and consider the negative power that your dismissal can create. For students to develop creative ideas, you need to withhold censorship. Your goal is to help students feel ownership and connection and become confident learners. You can reach these goals with any topic being investigated. The actual outcome of a project is not as relevant as the inquiry process.

Implementation

You can motivate question generation through any of three routes: directly observing interesting phenomena in a place (e.g., during exploration), thinking about issues that affect students' relationships or actions in a place, or obtaining background place knowledge from expert/traditional sources and wondering about things that remain unexplained.

During or after place exploration, engage students individually or in pairs through question generation activities. All students should participate in question generation. Students may be hesitant to pose questions if they are not often asked to do so or if they feel that their ideas are not good enough. Encourage a beginner mindset and emphasize the value of creativity. You should not yet judge any of the questions, except to provide positive affirmation.

Some activities to support question generation include:

- **Twenty questions activity**—Students explore the environment and write down any questions that come to mind within ten minutes.
- **Ten minutes of silence activity**—Students silently sit in one location for ten minutes and continuously record observations in their notebooks. Ensure that students are spaced apart so they do not distract each other.
- **Five senses observations**—Students write five categories on a sheet of paper or journal: sight, touch, smell, hearing, and tasting. As students explore, challenge them to make a set number of observations in each category. You will need to set parameters on tasting objects in the environment; you may need to know safe plants or other items in the environment that can be tasted.

- **Close observation activity**—Students observe an object closely for a specified period of time. Students should write down or draw observations and write a question linked to each observation.
- **Show and tell**—Students explore the place until they find a meaningful object or site. They then bring over the rest of the group and share what they are curious about there and why.
- **Use question templates**—For any of the previous scenarios, provide students with question templates (e.g., "Where does X happen?" "Why does X happen here, as opposed to there?" "How many of X is within a certain area?" "Does X affect Y?").
- **Tools**—Begin by thinking about what you can measure. Then have students focus on questions related to those measurements.

All questions should be written down or recorded. This supports formulating thoughts clearly and remembering ideas from one session to another.

Grade-Level Differentiation

Elementary (3–5)

Students may not be able to write down questions as fast as their ideas flow. You can instead write down questions for students on a whiteboard. Using a whole-class anchor chart (see Appendix 1) can be helpful. Notebooks are still useful for drawing, pressing leaves, or writing short observations. Students have short attention spans. Allowing physical movement and a lot of individual student freedom to explore or move at their own pace will help keep them engaged. Teacher-imposed transitions between steps for the youngest grades every few minutes will prevent students from getting bored or too involved with off-topic activities. Be careful not to interrupt students who are productively engaged.

Middle (6–8)

If you decide to allow each student or small group to select their own question, you will have to manage more, and likely different, projects.

On the other hand, students will be able to work on projects over longer periods of time, thus giving you more time to check in with each project.

High (9–12)

You can direct projects toward a specific topic area connected to other lessons being taught in the same year. However, it is important to still allow for creativity and student-led decisions to take place about project selection.

Examples

Urban schoolyard

- What color of the teachers' cars is the hottest and why?
- What do people do on the sidewalk?
- What do pigeons do all day long?

Suburban schoolyard

- Do ants poop?
- Do lizards live on trees or in the ground?
- Are all the leaves on a tree the same size?

Forest/lake area

- How many frogs live here?
- Why is the water brown?
- Does moss really grow on the north side of trees?
- Do animals stay away from trails or do they use them?
- How far away is the nearest star?

Developing a Question and Study Design

Figure 7.1 Brainstorming questions on sticky notes (here, a question about bananas with a book answer)

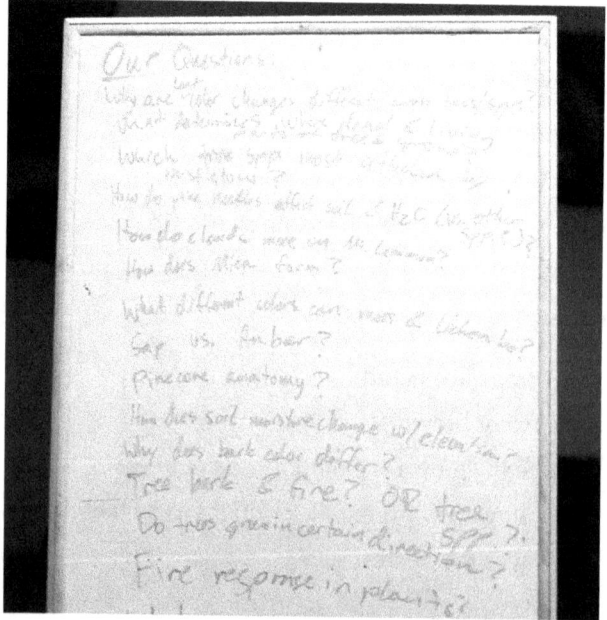

Figure 7.2 Sharing individually generated questions on a group whiteboard

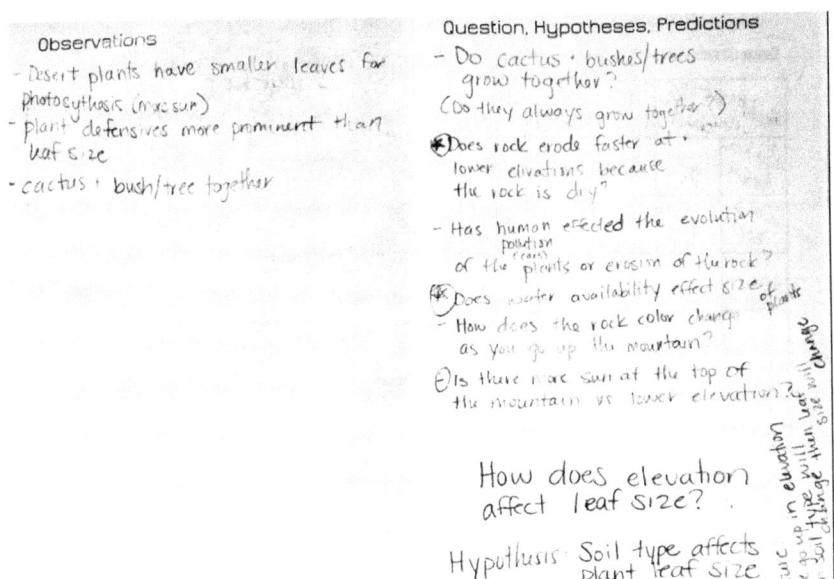

Figure 7.3 Starring questions that seem most interesting

7.2 Building a Strong Question

Concepts

The questions students generate usually will require refinement to become stronger. The basic requirements of a strong scientific question are:

- It is connected to the local place.
- Its answer is unknown.
- It has a possible answer: either alternative possibilities (i.e., at least two hypotheses) or a key descriptive aim can be specified (see later).
- Its answer can be found with a realistic amount of time, effort, and money.
- Its answer can be found ethically, without harming people or other organisms, the environment, or the place.

There will be many possible questions, but only time to answer one or a few. It is important to build consensus so that all group members feel motivated to find an answer to whatever question(s) are chosen.

Developing a Question and Study Design

Strong questions also provide opportunities for learning and engage all students. Questions can be very simple and still worthwhile (e.g., "How many birds live in the schoolyard?").

Some questions are more tractable than others. Generally, questions with descriptive answers are often the simplest to answer (e.g., those with "what," "where," "when," or "how many" phrasings). Questions with process-based answers (e.g., those with "why" phrasings) can often be broken up into specific sub-questions (e.g., those with "how" or "do" phrasings) that can be addressed via multiple hypotheses, and synthesized to answer the broader "why" question.

Weak questions often fall into common categories and can be redirected into strong questions by considering the following table.

Type of Weak Question	Rationale	Example Weak Question	Example Strong Question
Infeasible	Questions may require more time or resources than are available or may be unethical to answer. Redirect students to alternative questions.	1. What happens in a bee's brain as she chooses a flower? 2. Would an ant still be recognized by nestmates if she was washed with soap?	1. Do bees have preferences for flowers or a particular color? (Hypothesis-testing question) 2. Do ant trails ever connect different underground nests? (Descriptive question)
Answer can be looked up	An inquiry project is not needed to answer these questions. Redirect students to alternative questions.	1. What kind of rock is this? 2. What is a frog?	1. What types of rock can be found here? (Descriptive question) 2. Do tadpoles in a pond behave differently than fish in the same pond? (Hypothesis-testing question)

(continued)

Type of Weak Question	Rationale	Example Weak Question	Example Strong Question
Not connected to students' place	While these are strong questions, their answers do not relate to the focal place. Redirect students to ask questions about local places.	1. Do penguins in Antarctica spend more time on land or in the water? 2. What is the most explosive chemical and why?	1. Do birds in the schoolyard spend more time in the trees or sitting on buildings? (Hypothesis-testing question) 2. How much herbicide is used on lawns in different areas of the schoolyard? (Descriptive question)
Moral answer or not about the world as it exists	Science can answer questions about the world only as it is, not how it should be. However, it can study opinions. Redirect students to scientific questions, or frame questions as measuring opinions. Moral questions can be addressed in the reflection component of a project.	1. Should people be allowed to throw trash on the street? 2. Do animals believe in an afterlife?	1. Why is there more trash in some neighborhoods? (Hypothesis-testing question) 2. What do ants do if another ant dies? (Descriptive question)

Equity and Inclusion

Coming to consensus on a question can be difficult because the process is intimately tied to identity and power dynamics. Students of some identities may be less comfortable sharing questions or their motivations for asking them. Use facilitation approaches that empower all students to provide input, and set strong expectations for respectful and inclusive discourse (Chapter 6).

Implementation

After completing the question generation process, you can transition to the question winnowing process.

Have each student in each group share their questions with their peers and you. If you have too many questions, ask each student to only share their favorite one to three questions with the group. If a student is reluctant, allow them to pass with the understanding that you will come back to them. Write down all questions where all students can see them.

Next, ask students to use the previous criteria to determine which questions are strong ones. Also, ask them to think of whether or how they could strengthen each question, and allow them to do so. A think-pair-share can be helpful at this stage. Using such criteria to rule out questions helps groups make progress without students whose ideas were not chosen feeling left out. Your job is to act as a facilitator and guide, offering practical advice by asking questions (e.g., "How could you answer that question without a thermometer?" or "Would it be ethical to do that?").

It is not always obvious whether a question is tractable. The best way to find out is to allow your students to brainstorm the required study designs, hypotheses, and methods required. Thinking about the implications of hypotheses is critical—choosing a study design is thus an important component of the question selection process.

Once your students have identified a small set of strong questions, help them come to a consensus on which question they want to answer as a group. Ask them to discuss:

- Why the question is important or exciting to them
- Whether there is convergence in topic interest or methods among questions
- Whether everyone in the group would enjoy working on the question

Encourage students to work together to find consensus or compromise. Often the final question emerges as a combination of many students' ideas.

In rare cases, students may be disappointed that their idea was not chosen by the group. Returning to the question winnowing stage may allow a compromise to be found. If not, you may be able to help engage these students by giving them first choice of roles in the implementation of the project.

This consensus process will take an unknown amount of time, so build flexibility into your schedule. Patience is key because building consensus and engagement early on helps everything that comes afterward.

The process requires positive interpersonal dynamics to be successful, so you may also find it helpful to break up the question generation and winnowing process with additional team building or sense-of-place activities. You may also need to step in to guide the discussion or make hard choices, but it is better if you are able to step back.

Grade-Level Differentiation

Elementary (3–5)

Losing focus during question winnowing can occur. Use a whiteboard to guide discussion. Consider using larger groups so you can provide more support and facilitation. You can also be more direct in guiding question choice.

Middle (6–8)

Interpersonal dynamics may play a larger role in the winnowing process. Invest extra time in team building and facilitation.

High (9–12)

Give students full agency and responsibility to discuss and find consensus. Provide primarily technical advice to guide decisions.

Examples

Plants

- Do plants prevent soil from losing water?
- What microclimates are better for plant growth?
- How many different species of pollinators visit a flower?

Animals

- Do ants protect plants from being eaten?
- Do birds prefer to spend time closer to or farther from roads?
- Is macroinvertebrate diversity higher in streams when water moves faster?

Earth

- What kind of soil erodes fastest?
- Where is there the most pollution in the water?
- Does rock color influence how warm the rock gets?

People

- Do more affluent people have more plants in their yards?
- What environmental and human factors determine where people congregate in a park?
- Is the school's tap water safe to drink?

Developing a Question and Study Design

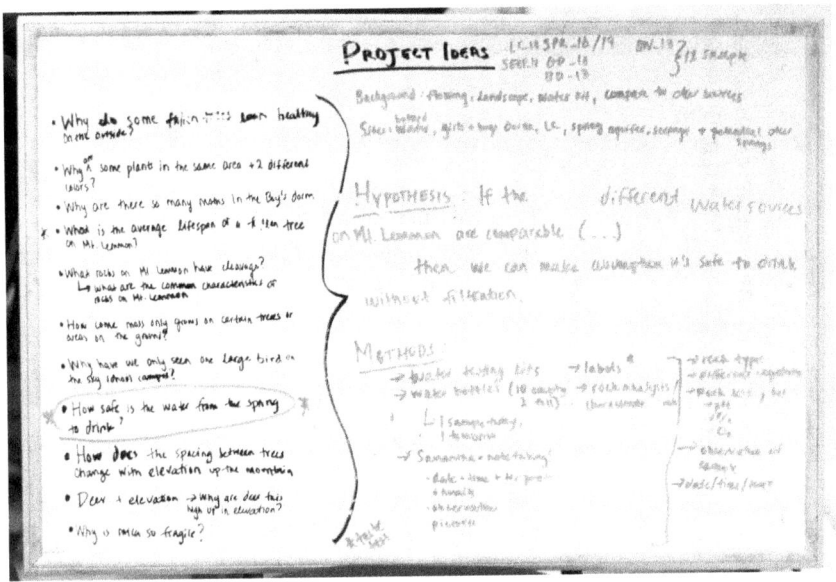

Figure 7.4 Selecting the strongest question (circled) by consensus

7.3 Designing a Study and Using an Anchor Chart

Concepts

Study design refers to determining what type of observations or data can answer a question. It is a creative process (Scheiner & Gurevitch, 2019).

To answer a question, a study's aim can either be descriptive or use hypothesis-testing methods. In a descriptive study, the specific and immediate measurements themselves are of greatest interest. In a hypothesis-testing study, the measurements help to distinguish between different answers. Descriptive studies are most appropriate when your goal is to characterize a phenomenon you do not know much about. Hypothesis-testing studies are most appropriate when your goal is to infer something that cannot be directly observed, such as an underlying mechanism. Both can lead to new knowledge about the world.

In both aims, one or two variables are measured: "something that needs explanation" (dependent variable or metric of interest, Y)

Developing a Question and Study Design

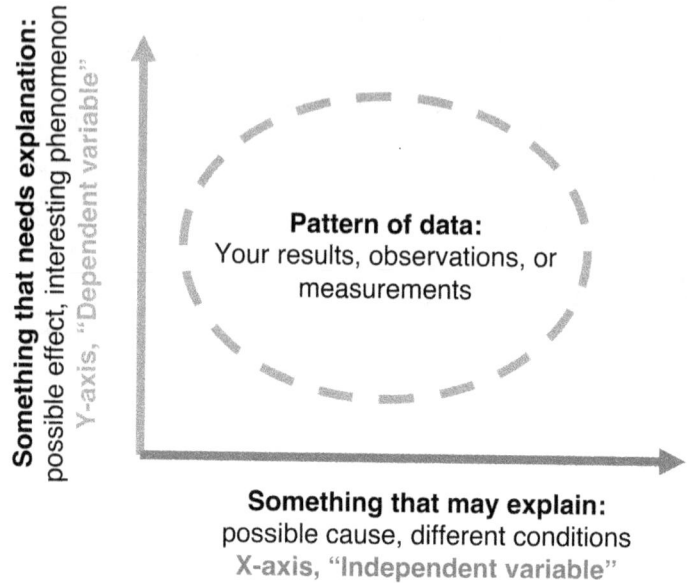

Figure 7.5 Generic graph template

and "something that may explain it" (independent variable or possible explanatory metric, X). The data (i.e., your measurements) will then illustrate whether or not the independent variable influences the dependent variable (i.e., the phenomenon of interest). In a hypothesis-testing study, prior ideas exist about how the variables are related; in a descriptive study, no prior ideas exist. The main focus in a descriptive study is the dependent variable; independent variables may be used to group the measurements for summarization (e.g., number of birds [dependent variable] in different parts of the schoolyard [independent variable]) or may be skipped (e.g., if the project is interested in the number of birds overall).

A hypothesis-testing study design will often fall into several common categories depending on logistical feasibility and ethics. However, any measurements or observations that allow you to confirm or refute the relationship between a dependent and independent variable can help test a hypothesis. The following table shows common study designs. The examples all address the question: "Do plants (of a particular species) grow better when they are well-watered?"

Developing a Question and Study Design

Name	How It Works	Dependent Variable (Y): Phenomenon of Interest That Needs Explaining	Independent Variable (X): Possible Explanation	Practical Considerations	Example Study
Randomized controlled trial (aka manipulative experiment)	• Identify replicate study units • Randomly assign different treatments (one treatment may be "do nothing", i.e., a "control") • Measure metric of interest for each unit	• Metric of interest for each unit	Categorical: which intervention (or none) was applied to each unit	• Experiments must be ethical and practical to do. • Only this design can rigorously identify causal relationships; the others identify correlations only	• After watering some plants and not others (X), measure plant size (Y) • Plot individual plants on strip plot, add bar for median or average
Cohort (aka before/after)	• Identify study units • Measure trait of interest • Wait for something to naturally happen to all units or apply the same intervention to all units • Measure metric of interest for each unit again	• Metric of interest for each unit; alternatively, calculate change (after-before) for each unit	Categorical: Before vs. after if showing original metric Alternatively, show a single category for difference Continuous: time points (group by before vs after)	If the event cannot be manipulated, may have to wait a long time for a response to occur	• Before and after a rainstorm (X), compare plant sizes (Y) • If categorical, plot individual plants on strip plot, add bar for median or average • If continuous, plot time series including before vs. after

(continued)

Name	How It Works	Dependent Variable (Y): Phenomenon of Interest That Needs Explaining	Independent Variable (X): Possible Explanation	Practical Considerations	Example Study
Cross-sectional (aka natural gradient)	• Identify study units in places that line up along a gradient • Measure how they differ in the metric of interest	Metric of interest for each unit	Categorical or continuous: Place on the gradient	May require visiting many locations	• In parts of the schoolyard that are near or far from a pond (X), compare plant sizes (Y) • Use a scatter plot for a continuous X or a strip plot for categorical X, adding bars for median or average
Case-control	• Identify study units that obviously exhibit ("cases") or don't exhibit ("controls") the phenomenon of interest • Then measure metrics of interest for each unit	Metric of interest for each unit	Categorical or continuous: The possible explanatory metric(s) for each unit	May be hard to find enough cases and controls in nature	• Find equal numbers of tall and short plants (Y) • Under each, collect soil and measure moisture content (X) • Plot as for cross-sectional design

Once a study design has been chosen, the types of analyses necessary to answer the question are straightforward. Each study design can be recast as yielding a certain type of graph. Most graphs plot two axes: the X-axis (left to right) depicts the independent variable, the Y-axis (bottom to top) depicts the dependent variable. Different types of data can be represented using different colors or multiple panels.

Each hypothesis yields a certain prediction for the graph type of interest. You can compare the data you collected to these expectations with visual interpretation or with statistical tests (Chapter 10); either process yields the answer to your question.

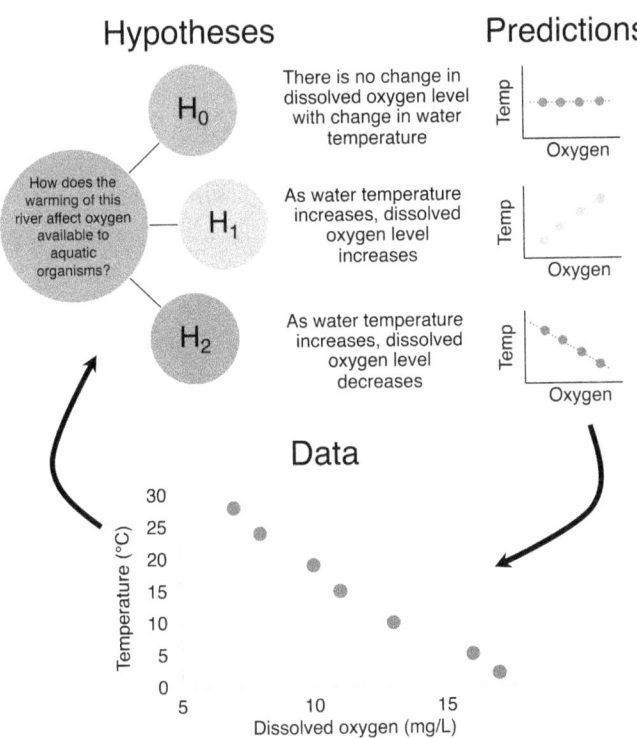

Figure 7.6 Example set of mutually exclusive hypotheses and predictions (top) that can be compared to data (bottom), rejecting Hypotheses 0 and 1

Developing a Question and Study Design

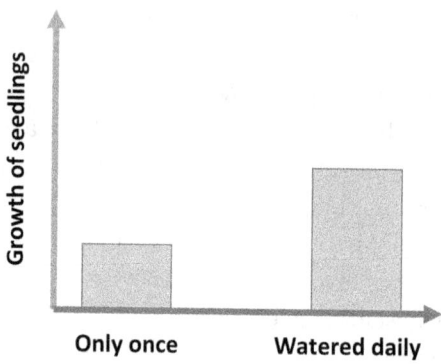

Figure 7.7 Example bar plot prediction for a randomized controlled trial design investigating plant growth

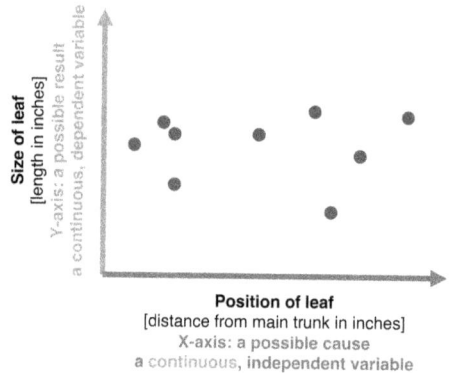

Figure 7.8 Example scatter plot prediction for a cross-sectional design investigating drivers of leaf size

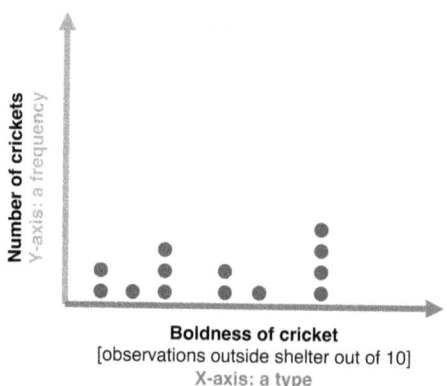

Figure 7.9 Example frequency plot prediction for a cohort design investigating cricket personalities

Question	Study Design	Independent Variable (X)	Dependent Variable (Y)	Data Points
Are insect pests a bigger problem at higher temperatures?	Cohort	Air temperature	Insect damage on plant leaves using a qualitative score	Measurements taken across the season
Do students focus more on moving or on resting during recess?	Case-control or cross-sectional	Behaviors (movement and rest)	Number of observations of students doing each behavior	Counts from several days or recess periods included
Do crickets have different personalities?	Descriptive	"Boldness" measured as time not in hiding	Number of crickets showing this behavior	Counts of how many crickets show each level of "boldness"

Implementation

First, consider whether the project should be descriptive (i.e., focused on exploration of directly observable things) or hypothesis-testing (i.e., focused on evaluating which of multiple possible answers is correct). This decision may depend on the age of your students and other considerations discussed in the next section. In a descriptive project, you can skip the hypotheses component of an anchor chart.

Second, consider different study designs. The choice will likely be determined by the practical considerations outlined earlier. You do not necessarily need to teach students terminology for study designs, but you should ensure they understand that intentional planning is required to obtain data that are useful for answering their question. In a hypothesis-testing study, some hypotheses may lend themselves more naturally to certain study designs (e.g., randomized controlled trials).

Third, you should explore different metrics to measure; that is, the particular variables that will appear on the graphs and that students will

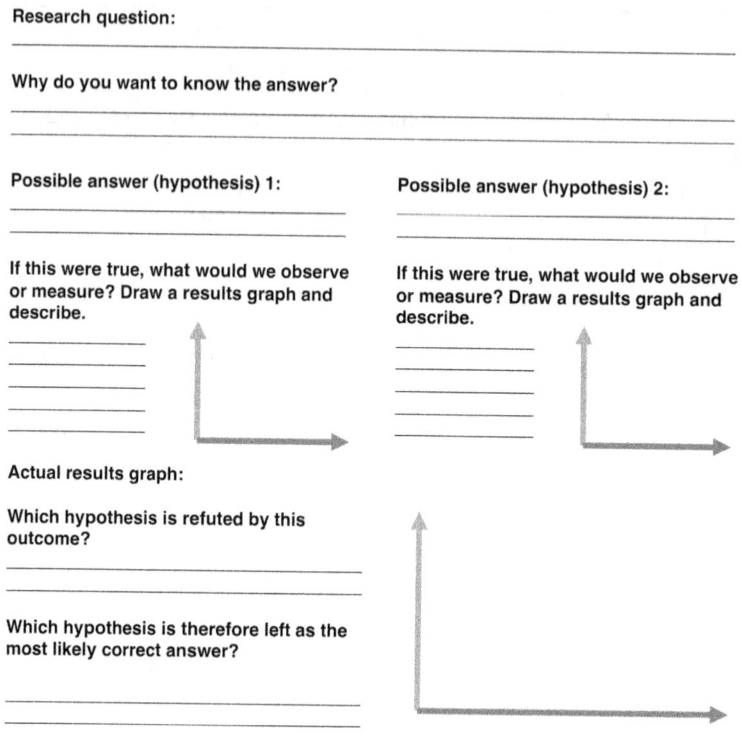

Developing a Question and Study Design

Research question:
_____

Why do you want to know the answer?
_____
_____

Possible answer (hypothesis) 1:
_____

Possible answer (hypothesis) 2:
_____

If this were true, what would we observe or measure? Draw a results graph and describe.

If this were true, what would we observe or measure? Draw a results graph and describe.

Actual results graph:

Which hypothesis is refuted by this outcome?
_____
_____

Which hypothesis is therefore left as the most likely correct answer?
_____

Figure 7.10 Generic anchor chart (see also Appendix A1.1)

physically measure. Sometimes these metrics are obvious (e.g., amount of water added to soil), while in other cases, they will require discussion (e.g., "plant growth" potentially represented by height, width, or number of leaves).

These steps can be structured using an anchor chart (see Appendix 1). The anchor chart indicates the flow of reasoning from question to hypotheses to predictions to data. Note that imagining different possible outcomes is a key and difficult part of this step. Later, this allows students to connect the data they collected back to the question they asked. By illustrating predictions visually as graphs, the anchor chart also streamlines later data analysis steps.

Each group can be given a blank anchor chart with the goal of filling in all the components they are certain about (e.g., a particular question, hypothesis, prediction, or measurement). Empty sections of the chart or places where there is not a clear item to fill in indicate places where students need to do additional thinking. The process is complete when the study design part of the chart is completely filled in and the information within it is internally consistent.

Ideas that do not fit into the chart can be flagged as unneeded, helping to minimize extraneous effort. An anchor chart also helps students recall their past work, especially when working on projects over multiple days, and allows them to make connections as new learning happens. When students present their findings later on, they can use the anchor chart to anticipate how they might organize and share their findings.

Encourage students to treat the chart iteratively. Sometimes, a question is decided first and then study designs are considered second. There should be a back-and-forth through the creative process. Have students work with pencils or erasable markers with their anchor charts to encourage this iterative process.

Grade-Level Differentiation

Elementary (3–5)

Minimize steps between measurements and interpretation. Students may suggest metrics of interest; you may have to suggest possible study designs. Use strip plots to display all data values and do not calculate summaries like averages. Continuous X-axis plots are more complex and will require additional practice.

Middle (6–8)

More of the study can be designed with active student participation. You can develop the anchor chart on a class whiteboard, so that while all students can contribute, you can keep control of the possibilities discussed and gently add information on possible graph types. Review the concept of scatter plots and practice finding the correct location for data points.

High (9–12)

Students can develop their own study design. Reviewing graph types is still useful.

Developing a Question and Study Design

Examples

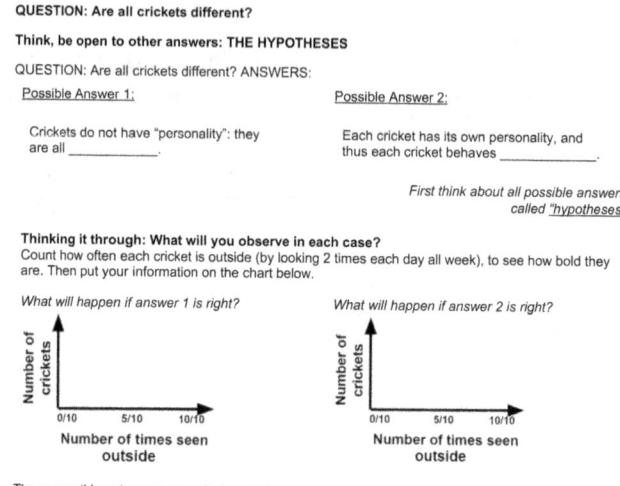

Figure 7.11 Example anchor chart for a cricket personality project, with study design predetermined by the teacher

Idea brainstorming: A third-grade teacher wanted to incorporate an inquiry-based group project in her unit on ecology, plants, and climate. They did not have any specific equipment or experience.

What could they measure? Around the school building were some (watered) grassy areas, some trees, and a bare desert area (not watered). From prior exploration with their class, they came up with the following list of possible measurements that could be included in a project with only a ruler, a thermometer, and the ability to count:

- Size of leaves
- Height of plants
- Temperature of the air
- Temperature of the ground
- Number of ants found in ten minutes
- Number of different types of animals seen in ten minutes
- Number of people crossing/using a particular area (e.g., during recess)

They realized there were some properties of locations that the students could assess:

- Ground shaded or not shaded
- Compass direction from the building or from a tree
- In the path of high walking traffic or not
- Land use form (e.g., lawn vs packed dirt vs natural desert landscape)

They realized that their class would be able to address several different questions, for example:

- Do trees help to create a cooler environment? (cross-sectional)
  - *Option 1*: air temperature (Y) under trees vs not under trees (X)
  - *Option 2*: ground temperature (Y) vs the height of plants (X)
- Is animal diversity or abundance impacted by land use? (Case-control)
  - *Option 1*: number of ants present (Y) on the artificial lawn vs the natural landscape fragments at the edge of the schoolyard (X)
  - *Option 2*: places with/without birds (Y) vs type of land cover in the schoolyard (X)

Other questions may be about the size of leaves on the same type of plant (e.g., grass or same type of tree) on different sides of the building to test whether leaf size responds to shading; does shade/air temperature affect the use of different schoolyard areas by students; does the temperature of the air reflect the ground temperature; is it better (cooler) to be in the shade of a tree than in the shade of a building; how much does the temperature of the ground or the air change across the school day; is a tree itself divided up into different microclimates.

7.4 Identifying Multiple Hypotheses and Predictions, or Not

Concepts

Hypotheses are plausible answers to the question you have posed or processes that explain the patterns you see. They are creative ideas originating with students and represent key engagement with the inquiry process.

Developing a Question and Study Design

Strong hypotheses help generalize your understanding of the world beyond your immediate observations. When you are starting out with inquiry-based projects, often both questions and hypotheses will be directly tied to visible or measurable phenomena (e.g., "Is the ground under the trees hotter than in the parking lot?"). The possible answers are simply "yes" or "no." However, when hypotheses contain more general ideas about the world, more learning and conceptual synthesis can occur. For example, if students start with the question posed earlier, you might guide them to expand on why the answer may be yes or no or why they are interested in this question. This could lead to the question, "Would planting trees help maintain a cooler city environment?" with at least three interesting hypotheses:

- **Hypothesis 1**—Yes, because trees shade the ground, leading to cooler temperatures
- **Hypothesis 2**—Yes, because trees evaporate water, leading to cooler temperatures
- **Hypothesis 3**—No, because the air moves sufficiently to cause the temperature to be the same across at least the entire schoolyard

These hypotheses are connected to Disciplinary Core Ideas and would potentially allow generalization to other places.

Hypotheses also need to make predictions (i.e., correctly anticipating previously unknown results). A prediction is what you expect the data to look like if the hypothesis is true, not what you imagine will actually happen. Predictions may be shown as graphical representations or statements like "X should be smaller than Y" or "when X increases, Y increases too." Predictions are logical consequences of each hypothesis, such that if they do not happen, the hypothesis can be considered false. Useful predictions are ones that help distinguish between hypotheses. If all your hypotheses make the same prediction, then this prediction is not useful for answering your question. The predictions you make identify the potential measurements that should be made. If variables do not appear in predictions, then they do not need to be measured. Alternatively, if an unaccounted-for variable seems interesting, then the hypotheses and predictions might need to be revised to include it.

Multiple hypotheses need to be allowed to compete against each other; this also implies that you always have at least two contradictory predictions.

If there is only one hypothesis, then there is no way to empirically determine if another answer might be better. You should never have just one hypothesis that you are trying to "prove." This creates bias in the study, emotional attachment to a specific outcome, and potential resistance to accepting the actual outcome if a hypothesis turns out to be "wrong." A set of hypotheses should even include answers initially deemed unlikely. All interesting answers should be considered, even if not all can be tested in the project.

Hypotheses are tested by comparing their predictions to reality via "strong inference." You are only able to make strong inferences when you "rule out" rather than "rule in" hypotheses (Fuller, 2004; Platt, 1964). Any hypothesis which yields a prediction that does not agree with the data is "ruled out" (i.e., rejected). Any hypothesis not rejected is typically accepted (we say, "The study supports the hypothesis" or, more accurately, "The study cannot rule out the hypothesis"). It is possible that this inversion process (accepting as true the only hypotheses that are not ruled out) may sometimes produce erroneous inferences, so some caution is required in interpreting any hypothesis-testing study. It is also possible that all of the hypotheses you think of are ruled out by the data; this implies that you did not consider all possible answers. Several hypotheses may be ruled out at once if they made the same prediction; this should be avoided by ensuring you have enough hypotheses so that contradictory predictions are produced.

Inference is based on the data alone, not on opinion or desire. Data can include all the information you collected according to your study design, as long as you did not know what it would be as you drew up the hypotheses and predictions. Data can include direct or received human experience of the world (for example, consultation of elders or other community members).

The art of hypothesis formulation consists of identifying possible answers to your question that refer to interesting, general processes, while making concrete, realistically testable, and hopefully mutually exclusive predictions. This process requires creativity and anticipating both what can be measured and how actual measurements will be compared to predictions.

Some hypotheses may yield predictions that are unethical or impractical to test (e.g., involving violence or equipment you do not have). A study does not compare every prediction to reality, but it is critical to acknowledge these hypotheses as untested alternatives when doing strong inference.

Alternatively, descriptive studies are often used when you do not yet know enough about a phenomenon to even state any hypotheses. Such inquiry that focuses on exploration alone (i.e., without testing hypotheses) is also valuable and important. These inquiries expand curiosity, connection to place, and factual knowledge. Descriptive questions can support learning in terms of sharpening natural history and observation skills, analyzing data, and developing communication and teamwork skills. Students can also develop the same sense of ownership and actualization as with a hypothesis-driven question.

Descriptive studies can be a starting point to guide students to later hypothesis-driven studies. Observations provide a key foundation for science. Without exploration and observation of phenomena, you cannot build up to a more general understanding of processes necessary for formulating mechanistic hypotheses. Concepts and ideas about mechanisms can be built on top of observations later.

Equity and Inclusion

Scientific inquiry can appear to devalue knowledge that cannot be reduced to data or graphs and can hide underlying discussions of what *should be*. Other fields like philosophy, religion, and spirituality are concerned with how the world ought to be, what goals people should have, and what is morally good. Scientific inquiry cannot answer these types of questions (confusion about this point is often termed the "is-ought problem" or the "naturalistic fallacy"). Science can, however, be used to determine what and how people think about the world. Discussing what the world is like now, rather than what it could be, does not preclude broader learning in additional educational contexts, and in broader reflection (Chapter 11).

Implementation

Once students have started their anchor chart (see Appendix 1) and potentially selected a study design, have them brainstorm possible answers to the question. Include answers that come from prior knowledge, but also include unlikely or silly ones. List them all. Then go through the list systematically, filtering down to a smaller set of hypotheses that seem comprehensive but distinct.

After hypotheses are identified, shift students toward making predictions. Ask, "How would you know if that hypothesis was false? What evidence would convince you?" to stimulate a creative discussion of possible observations or experiments. Because hypotheses can only be ruled out rather than ruled in, think of predictions that would be inconsistent with each hypothesis. Go through this process for each hypothesis. Being open-minded at this stage is important.

Students benefit from drawing mock graphs that visualize predictions. Encourage students to be explicit about the axes of the graph and how they will be measured. These graphs also provide a framework, or "mental picture," for designing the methodology for the study and guiding future data analyses. Verbal predictions are good starting points (e.g., "I think A will get bigger if B is bigger") and can often then be transformed into graphs appropriate for the study design (e.g., a scatter plot of B vs A).

Predictions are not what you deem likely to happen, but what needs to happen for a hypothesis not to be ruled out; thus, you must have contradictory predictions for the same measurements for the different hypotheses. Making predictions enables students to identify the variables they need to observe or manipulate in their study. Useful predictions can be qualitative (e.g., "If trees cool the ground, then soil temperature under a tree should be lower than in the open") or quantitative (e.g., "If only gravity acts on an object, then the speed of a dropped object will be proportional to the falling time").

Alternatively, students can think about the equipment they have on hand to identify possible variables they could observe or manipulate. They can then use this list to think of possible predictions that link these variables together. Proxies can be used for variables that are difficult to measure (e.g., "playground use" could become "number of students on the swings"). Iterate through this process until students have at least two hypotheses that produce different predicted patterns on the same graph, where the graph includes quantities that are feasible to measure.

Sample Question	Concept/Theory	Sample Hypotheses	Sample Predictions
	Idea upon which the hypotheses are based	Explanation of phenomenon	Expected outcome
Does soil moisture affect leaf temperature?	Evaporation of water is how many organisms regulate their temperature; this may depend on water availability. On the other hand, if plants do not regulate evaporation, leaf temperature may be determined by conditions near the leaf	Plants regulate leaf temperature: 1. Soil moisture decreases plant leaf temperature 2. Plant leaf temperature depends on the species of plant Plants do not regulate leaf temperature: 3. Leaf temperature depends only on air temperature 4. Leaf temperature depends only on whether the leaf is in the sun	If we measure leaf temperature in a series of plants, some of which were supplemented with water and some were not, then: 1. Predicts watered plants have cooler leaves 2. Predicts that temperature differs between species 3. Predicts that watering and species have no effect, but leaf temperature correlates with ambient temperature 4. Predicts that watering and species have no effect, but leaves in direct sunlight are hotter than those in the shade

(continued)

Developing a Question and Study Design

Sample Question	Concept/Theory Idea upon which the hypotheses are based	Sample Hypotheses Explanation of phenomenon	Sample Predictions Expected outcome
Does the presence of insect predators influence pollinator behavior?	Flying pollinators have very good vision and can detect predators on flowers. Crab spiders are predators of insects that often wait or prey on flowers	1. Predator presence reduces pollinator visits to flowers 2. Pollinators select flowers based on the flower's traits, not based on the presence of predators	If we measure number of pollinator visits to flowers with and without a small plastic spider (or spider shape cutout) on them, hypothesis: 1. Predicts that flowers with the plastic spider receive fewer visits 2. Predicts the number of visits to each flower type is the same
Can birds use cacti in the way that they use trees (e.g., mesquite or palo verde trees)?	While palo verde trees and mesquite trees are very similar in structure, cacti are very different and have many defenses. Therefore, there might be differences in how and which birds use these plants	1. Birds have no preference between palo verde and mesquite trees. 2. All birds prefer to perch on trees over cacti 3. Only small birds prefer to perch on cacti	If we observe several trees and cacti each for the same amount of time: 1. Predicts that the number and size of birds landing on trees is the same as for cacti 2. Predicts that more birds land on trees than cacti, but their sizes are the same 3. Predicts that the average size of birds landing on cacti is smaller than that of birds landing on trees

Developing a Question and Study Design

Grade-Level Differentiation

Elementary (3–5)

Students need more guidance about what can be measured and how. Confronting students with problems that are too hard, abstract, or outside of their experience will lead them to lose focus and confidence. You may want to suggest specific study designs in response to student questions. Given a planned results graph, students can often come up with the predictions for each hypothesis. Students may try to guess, or claim to know from background knowledge, what the outcomes will be; remind them that all possible outcomes need to be imagined.

Middle (6–8)

Students are more able to focus on a problem for longer, and more of the process of figuring out *how* a question can be answered can be student-driven. Nonetheless, you may want to suggest study designs after students select questions.

High (9–12)

Creative decisions about what variables should be measured can be assigned to students. Students will likely need support in evaluating various possible study designs and may need clear definitions of what equipment or materials are accessible or what budget can be used.

Developing a Question and Study Design

Examples

Figure 7.12 A single-hypothesis study (fourth grade). An alternative hypothesis was likely considered but was not stated by the students

times each day all week), to see how bold they are. Then we put all crickets on this chart below.

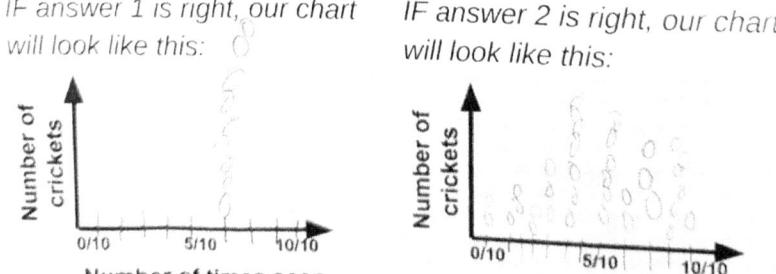

Scientists call these possible outcomes <u>predictions</u>.

Figure 7.13 A two-hypothesis study (third grade; see Figure 7.8)

Developing a Question and Study Design

Figure 7.14 A three-hypothesis study (fifth grade)

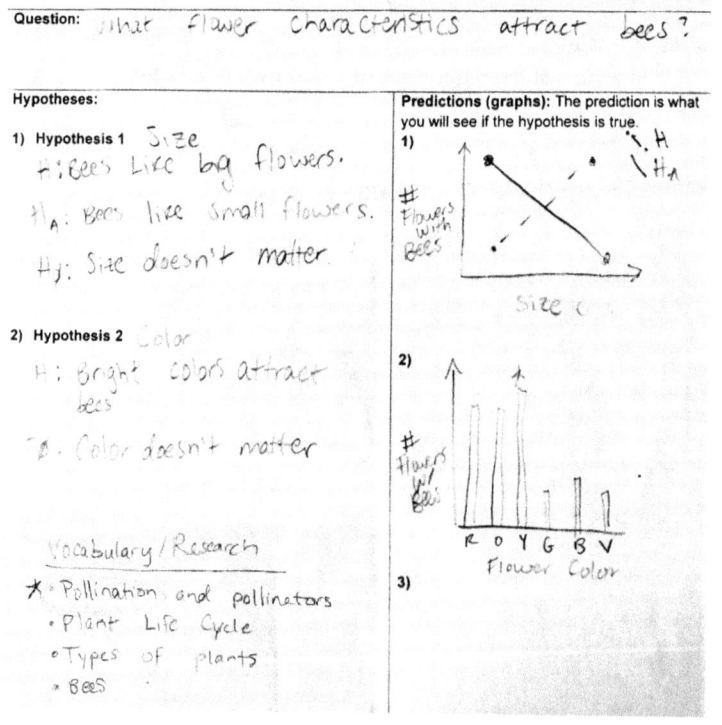

Figure 7.15 A five-hypothesis study (middle school)

Developing a Question and Study Design

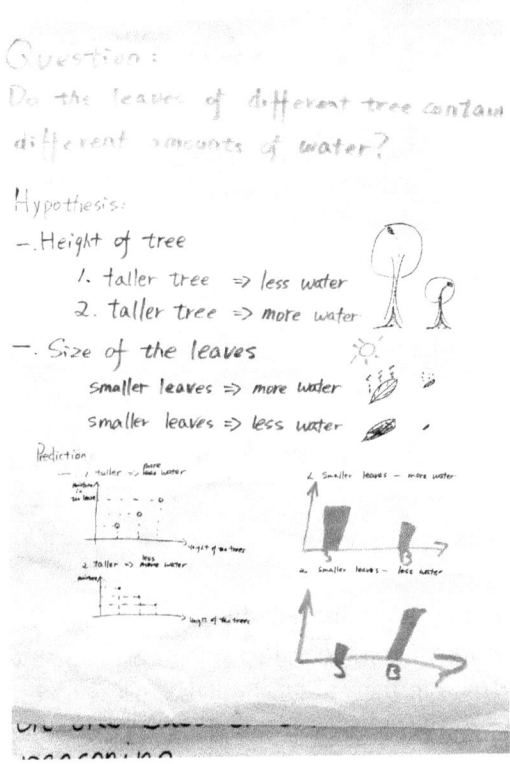

Figure 7.16 A four-hypothesis study (high school)

 Planning Data Collection

8.1 Choosing How Much to Measure

Concepts

After identifying predictions and variables, you should decide how much work to invest in measuring them. Repeating measurement multiple times increases confidence in the resulting values. This is a critical lesson that should be taken away from any inquiry project: any measurements you make are only estimates of the true value. Making more measurements improves your estimate, no matter where the uncertainties come from. Any one measurement is affected not only by measurement error but also by many factors that are unknown and often unknowable. However, you do not need to know what these factors are, nor do you need to eliminate them; you only need to make multiple measurements and summarize them by taking an average.

For example, suppose you were trying to estimate the average height of all the students in your school. If you measured only a single student, you might (by chance) have chosen a very tall student; taking this as an estimate for the height of students generally would lead you to overestimate how tall students typically are. If you measure three or four students, you will likely (by chance) sample data from some short and tall students, so that your estimate of the average height begins to be more accurate. Eventually, if you sample all of the students in your school, you will arrive at the true average height. However, it is probably not practical to measure every single student in the school, so you will stop sampling at some point and decide that your estimate is a good representation of the true value.

Similarly, if you do a randomized controlled trial and only apply the control once and the treatment once, you cannot be sure that any difference between the groups is the result of the treatment and not of one of the many unknown factors that affect each measurement. Sometimes single pieces of extraordinary evidence would be sufficient to reject a hypothesis (e.g., the observation of a single alien would reject an aliens-do-not-exist hypothesis), but these scenarios likely will not arise in student projects.

Determining the appropriate number of repeat measurements (i.e., "sample size") is challenging. In practice, you will probably make the decision based on estimating available time and resources more than statistical considerations. For example, if you only have an hour to make measurements, your sample size will be smaller than if data collection takes place over a week; if you are measuring the height of trees in the schoolyard, you will make fewer measurements than if you are measuring the size of leaves. Additionally, the variability in your measurement (from a variety of unknown factors and errors) is probably larger than you expect. Thus, plan to make as many measurements as time allows.

Implementation

Confidence in results depends on how you replicate measurements. For example, consider the experiment where you are measuring rock temperatures. You could measure the temperature for different types of rocks, then your conclusion would apply across rock types. Or you could measure the same rock but on different days, for a conclusion that applies over time but not to different rocks. You could even replicate the measurement just on the same rock over a short time for more confidence that the variability does not come from the thermometer or student not measuring consistently. Generally, the wider you spread your measurements (across time, space, type, observers), the more generally applicable your conclusions will be. You typically should not attempt to hold constant any of the factors that lead to varying measurements (e.g., which student does the measuring or at what time you measure)—this will decrease variability but also reduce generalizability.

The accuracy of your overall conclusion thus depends on the number of samples you can get, but it also depends on how evenly or randomly you can spread them out across irrelevant factors. If your rule of picking a particular measurement is in any way biased toward particular outcomes, then your outcomes will be biased and not generalize well. For example, returning to the task of measuring the temperature of rocks, you should try to pick the rocks measured randomly with respect to what temperature they are. If you avoid measuring hot rocks because they hurt to touch, then your estimates of rock temperature will be lower than they should be.

Once a sampling plan has been proposed, ask students to determine how long each measurement will likely take, inclusive of setup and staying focused and travel time (e.g., ten minutes each). You may need to let them try the method or equipment to get a good sense of this. Divide the total time available by this value for the maximum number of possible samples (e.g., 2 hours/15 minutes = 8 measurements at most).

A simple solution is to obtain as many samples as possible in the time available. However, if this number is smaller than the desired number, then encourage students to determine what trade-offs they need to make; for example:

- Can you work with fewer sites?
- Can you work with fewer data points?
- Can you change the protocol to work faster?
- Do you need to change the question?

Come to a final proposal after a round of iteration. Large sample sizes may not be possible when each measurement is slow (e.g., a study of soil that requires digging a large hole) or because replicates do not exist (e.g., a study of flower color where there is only one yellow flower in the schoolyard). Do not discourage students when their sample sizes are small.

Grade-Level Differentiation

Elementary (3–5)

Focus on the overall pattern of results while presenting intrinsic variability in measurements as real, not erroneous.

Middle (6–8)

Introduce more quantitative concepts, like graphing a frequency distribution. Students may also be able to collect larger sample sizes. Maintain your focus on the overall pattern of results, and present data variation as real, not erroneous.

Planning Data Collection

High (9–12)

As noted earlier.

Examples

Figure 8.1 Consulting a map to determine how many sites can be realistically sampled when walking between them

Data collection: Observe your cricket. Put a checkmark in a house if you think it is in the shelter. Put a checkmark next to the house if you see the cricket outside of the shelter. Do not make any new checkmarks if your cricket is dead.

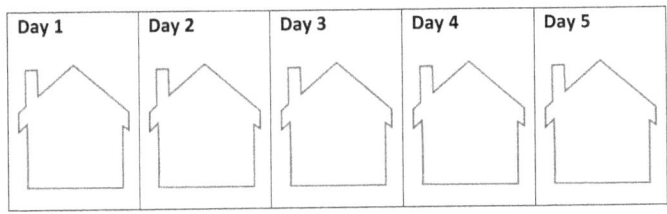

Figure 8.2a Teacher-provided datasheet for making multiple cricket behavior observations (third grade; see Figure 7.8)

175

Planning Data Collection

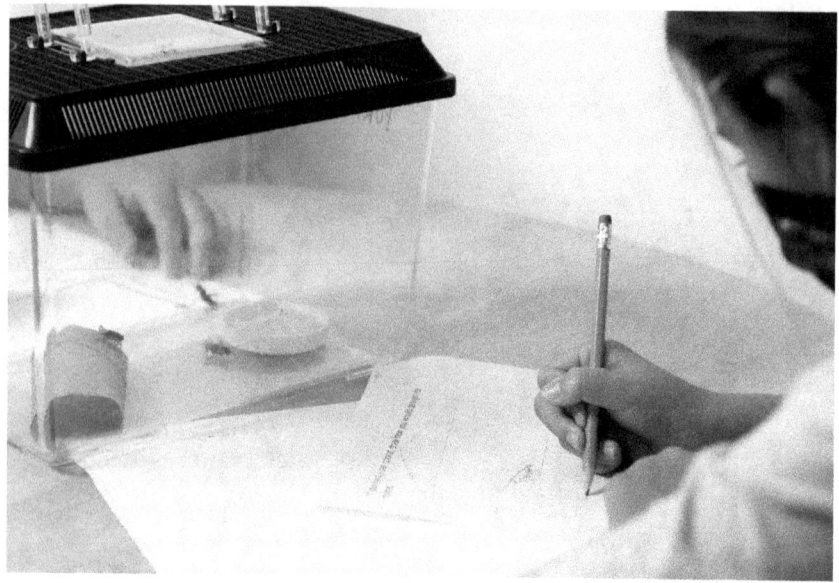

Figure 8.2b Students observing crickets

8.2 Choosing What to Do (Protocols, Checklists, and Datasheets)

Concepts

Being organized early on prevents confusion and chaos once outside. Once groups have chosen a question and identified variables, it is useful to plan how those variables will be measured by creating a protocol, a checklist of necessary equipment, and a datasheet for recording observations. A protocol ensures consistent data collection and provides an opportunity to decide on statistical and practical aspects of data collection. It helps students reach a consensus on their roles and the necessary tasks and acts as a reference point for check-ins. The checklist of necessary items helps students use outside time effectively by not forgetting or losing equipment. Making a datasheet ahead of time ensures students have thought carefully about what they need to record.

Equity and Inclusion

There are often many ways to collect data to answer a single question. This means there is much opportunity to develop protocols that maximize student accessibility. Make sure that every student is able to have a meaningful and distinct role in data collection.

Implementation

For a protocol, have students write out a set of numbered steps they will take to carry out their study. Steps should indicate what they are going to do, what they are going to use to do it, how many times it will be done, and what will be done with the collected data (see template in Appendix 1). Have students write down what units of measurement they plan to record and their goal for the number of samples or observations necessary. To ensure the steps of the protocols align with the allotted time, you can ask students to approximate how much time they expect each step will take. Leave room in protocols to make notes about problems and what was done to solve them.

Ask students to review the protocol to determine if it is:

- **Inclusive**—All students are participating.
- **Ethical**—The work is not too harmful to any people, organisms, or the environment.
- **Feasible**—There is enough time and equipment available.

Make changes until all three criteria are met.

After developing a protocol, have students make a checklist of all of the equipment they will need to implement the protocol. Once they know what they will do and what they need to implement the protocol, have students make their own datasheet. This is not a trivial task, as many students may not have made their own table for data collection before. It is helpful to have a header on datasheets where the date, observers, and location can be recorded and to label all variables with units (see template in Appendix 1). Observations can then be recorded in a table with variables arranged as columns and observations as rows. The datasheet itself can be hand-drawn in notebooks or typed on a spreadsheet.

Technology such as tablets or phones may be used to collect data either through direct entry of observations into spreadsheets or by recording digital data (e.g., sounds or photographs). Digital data may be used for quantification or identification (e.g., insects or plants) or simply to document protocols. If students propose to collect digital data, they should include a system for naming and organizing digital files in their protocol.

Grade-Level Differentiation

Elementary (3–5)

To keep students on task and ensure that recorded information is useful and consistent over time, use a structured datasheet that requires minimal reading and writing. A datasheet makes the data collection plan explicit in all its details. Support will be needed to help translate the plan from the anchor chart into a suitable datasheet.

Middle (6–8)

Students can take more responsibility in planning the details of their data collection. They can design their own datasheet and discuss what needs to be included. Collaboration between groups can allow for students to provide and receive feedback on their plans.

High (9–12)

As noted earlier.

Planning Data Collection

Examples

Figure 8.3 Learning to use a digital weather meter

8.3 Choosing Roles

Concepts

Each member of the team will contribute in different ways. Students should decide in advance who will do what on each team to maximize the effectiveness of outside time and to avoid conflict.

Equity and Inclusion

Consider having students switch roles regularly to avoid any one person dominating.

Implementation

Assigning roles can be done as part of the protocol development process. Ask students to identify different roles that might be useful (e.g., someone measures X, someone measures Y). Remind students they also may want to have people responsible for other key roles including:

- **Explorer**—Locates sites, organisms, or objects
- **Welfare checker**—Reminds others to eat snacks, drink water, and use the toilet
- **Data recorder**—Writes down measurements
- **Timer**—Keeps track of overall schedule
- **Equipment keeper**—Carries equipment
- **Artist**—Documents projects

Depending on group size, some students may have more than one role or share a role. Some roles may seem more exciting than others, so conflict can occur. First, let students pick roles based on their preferences and stated skills. If there is conflict, you can suggest that students rotate between roles or share a role. Alternatively, you can encourage students to take an unwanted role by highlighting its major contribution to team success.

Planning Data Collection

Examples

Figure 8.4 Students in self-selected roles, from left to right: tree finder, tape runner, number reader, site describer

Figure 8.5 Data recorder

Planning Data Collection

Figure 8.6 Illustrator

Collecting Data Outside

9.1 Practicing Collecting Data

Concepts

Students typically have limited prior experience collecting or recording data, using equipment, learning outside, or managing the flow of a project. Confusion, conflict, or disempowerment can occur if students are expected to perform immediately at a high level when carrying out their projects. This can be exacerbated if there is a fixed and small amount of time that students have to be outside (e.g., if you only have bus transport for one day) or if students feel time pressure. To increase student confidence, you should emphasize the importance of working together as a team, learning to use equipment, and following their protocol.

Equity and Inclusion

Ensure all the students who want to learn how to do a particular task get a chance. Interpersonal dynamics within a group during practice are likely to be repeated when outside, so be prepared to use facilitation skills to mitigate any issues early on.

Implementation

During or after the protocol development process, provide training on safe use of equipment, then allow students to play with or practice with the equipment they will ultimately use. Have student teams do a test run of their data collection process. Students can practice in the classroom or the schoolyard, substituting features of these places (if needed) for the features they expect to find in the focal place.

Changes will likely be necessary, so provide time for students to revise their documents. Students often find that their plans are too ambitious or complex. They may need to reduce sample sizes or reduce the number of measurements they make. Set an expectation that iterative refinement is normal.

Before starting, set the norms that mistakes and errors are expected and that practice and iteration are needed to develop data collection skills. You should circulate between groups to facilitate their learning; expect to spend at least a few minutes with each group. This is a key point for you to request and use adult volunteers to provide active support to students.

Expect to spend at least a half hour on practice. This time will be repaid with more efficient use of time later.

Grade-Level Differentiation

Elementary (3–5)

Students will need more initial support and direction, including team building activities and practicing observation skills.

Examples

Figure 9.1 Practicing using a quadrat in the schoolyard

Figure 9.2 Practicing recording data in the classroom

9.2 Collecting Data

Concepts

Data collection is the heart of a project where students can feel closest to the places they are studying. Providing space and time to collect data can be critical for developing connection to place and confidence in students.

When your students go outside, set clear expectations around organization and structure to ensure that students stay focused and that they follow the plans they have made in the classroom. However, you also should provide sufficient freedom for students to feel they can make the place their own and that they are empowered to collect the data they feel they need.

Apparent failure can occur during data collection (e.g., nothing interesting is observed, the protocol does not work, measurements take too long, or equipment breaks). Encourage students about the value of the inquiry process itself and the value of *all* results; for example, recording a zero to indicate an event was not observed may still be valid and informative. Or redirect students to simpler versions of a question, related questions, or simpler methods. A small step backward can support a bigger step forward.

Serendipity can also occur during data collection. When students make observations or have experiences that are outside the domain of their plans, they may come to new and valuable perspectives. Oftentimes the things you are not looking for are the most interesting. Staying open to the unexpected can be supported by integrating observation through the data collection process and also by communicating a supportive attitude toward surprises.

Implementation

Set expectations for behavior and ground rules for space and time used before starting work. Use your risk management plan to keep safety in mind (see Appendix 2) and explain the rationale for any safety-related boundaries. It is often helpful to set a schedule for data collection with formalized breaks and check-ins when you will visit each group (e.g., you will visit each group at least once, or students have to reconvene as a large group after 30 minutes). Breaks can be opportunities to regroup and participate in sense of place (Chapter 5) or team building activities (Chapter 6), or to share obstacles and preliminary observations.

Be prepared for some behavior challenges and invest time in addressing them (Chapter 6). Floating between groups is vital in determining which groups have students fulfilling their roles, which are comfortable, and which are collecting data. Investing further time in team building and sense-of-place activities can be a good investment immediately before data collection so that teams function smoothly and with motivation for being outside.

Ask students to use notebooks to keep data records, following the template datasheet they developed with their protocols. Additionally, encourage students to document all their observations during their study, especially for surprising data points or to documents interesting observations beyond the inquiry question or study design. If collecting digital data (e.g., photographs, sound recordings), students can use their notebooks or datasheets to keep track of file names and content.

Have a system to keep track of equipment. Use checklists to determine whether all equipment has been accounted for before and after going outside, do a "roll call" of items and ask members of each group to hold up items as called, or make individuals responsible for particular items.

Common problems to be aware of during data collection include:

- **Lost equipment**—It is very easy for students to misplace equipment. Use brightly colored equipment or use brightly colored tape to mark your tools. It can also be helpful to package equipment in backpacks or plastic tubs.

- **Lost notebooks/pencils**—Students also often lose their notebooks and pencils. Have extras available. Consider collecting notebooks at break times or the end of a full day.
- **Bad handwriting**—Bad handwriting can prevent data from being usable. Check in on data recording frequently.
- **Paper damage**—Be careful if students are working near water, fire, or wind. All of these can easily destroy notebooks and, by extension, data.
- **Equipment misuse**—Students can unintentionally misuse equipment, especially if it is the first time they are using a new item. Common issues include reading inches instead of centimeters on rulers, failing to zero out balances/scales, and reading decimal points in the wrong places. Students can also intentionally misuse equipment (e.g., using magnifying glass to start fires).

Some common data recording techniques include:

- **Tick marks**—When counting numbers of objects (e.g., insects on flowers), it is often easier for students to sequentially count using tick/tally marks rather than directly writing down numbers.
- **Codes**—When recording data for different types of objects (e.g., types of rocks), it can be useful to use codes to enable faster data recording. For example, granite could be G and sandstone S.
- **Morphonames**—When recording data for unknown types of objects (e.g., insect species), you can give unique labels to each distinct type (e.g., "big orange wing [BOW]" for a monarch butterfly, "white with gray dots [WGD]" for a cabbage moth). This will allow identification at a later date and time without slowing data collection. Additionally, determining scientific names may not be necessary for the inquiry question.

Common sampling techniques include:

- **Randomization**—To remove bias from the selection of a site, randomize distances or directions. A blindfolded student can be twirled around several times, then walk several steps, or toss a stick to select a site.
- **Quadrat**—Pick a fixed sample area (e.g., a 1 × 1 m box) and count all the objects in the sample area. Then divide the number of objects by the area you sampled, and multiply by the total area (e.g., the area of the schoolyard) to get an estimate of the total count.

Collecting Data Outside

- **Transect**—Pick a fixed sample length (e.g., a 10 m line) and walk along it. Count all objects within a certain distance from the line (e.g., 0.5 m). Then divide the number of objects by the length and width of the transect line (here, 10 × (2 × 0.5) = 10 m²), and multiply by the total area of the study area to get an estimate of the total count. If you do not have a measuring tape, you can use a rope to accomplish the same goal. Tying knots in the rope or drawing tick marks with a permanent marker at regular intervals allows counting distances. Student body lengths are also useful length units that can later be converted into standard units.

Grade-Level Differentiation

Elementary (3–5)

Use short, structured intervals of data collection interspersed with check-ins, interpretation, or question-answer activities. Groups can also regularly rotate between the areas if enough adults are present.

Examples

Figure 9.3 Using a whiteboard for group data recording

Collecting Data Outside

Figure 9.4 Measuring flow speed by floating leaves down a stream and timing their progress

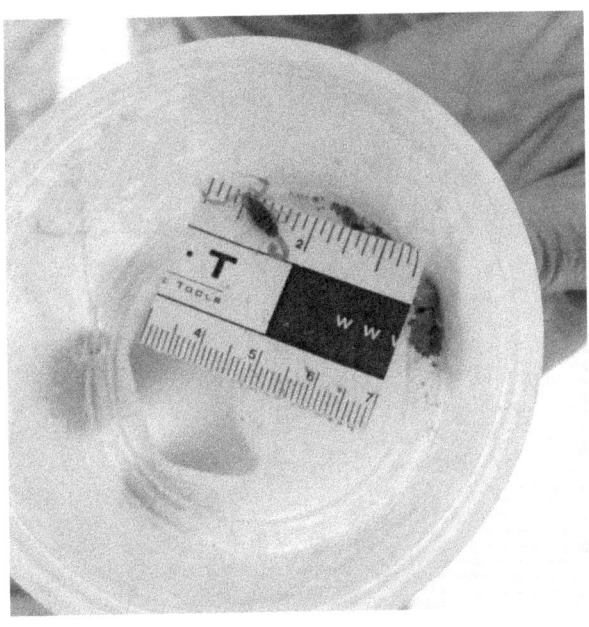

Figure 9.5 Safely measuring scorpion length in a plastic tub

Collecting Data Outside

Figure 9.6 Collecting stream macroinvertebrates in ice cube trays

Figure 9.7 Measuring soil temperature with a meat thermometer within a quadrat

Collecting Data Outside

Figure 9.8 Storing soil samples in plastic bags

Figure 9.9 Setting up a vegetation transect with a tape

Collecting Data Outside

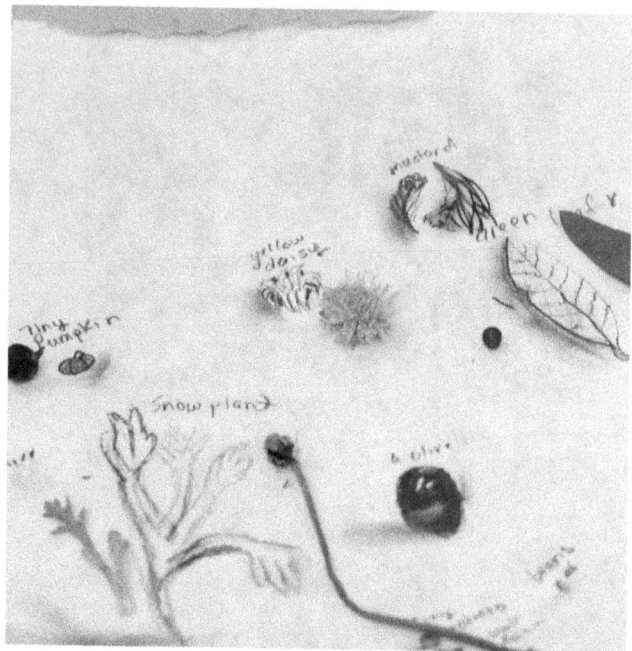

Figure 9.10 Identifying species by morphoname

9.3 Securing Data

Concepts

Data are not always ready for analysis and interpretation by a group because they may exist only in one student's notebook or contain errors. It is important to copy the data to a safe and shared location, then carry out quality checks before using it. During this process, it may become clear that additional data collection or changes in protocol are needed. Analyses are only as good as the data used to carry them out.

Implementation

Find a quiet area where students will be comfortable. Then copy all the data to a common and safe location. Students can use a whiteboard or poster paper to copy information. If useful, one student can read out data and another can transcribe it. If computers are available, use a shared spreadsheet file or shared folder.

Ensure you keep a copy of the raw data or notebooks in case students need to revisit them later. This might involve photocopying datasheets, collecting notebooks, or sharing photographs of datasheets using a phone camera.

Next, have students organize the data. If an anchor chart was used (Appendix 1), there should already be a natural structure for the data. If not, ask students to create one by asking them:

- What variables were measured?
- How can these variables be related to, or paired with, each other?
- What structure would be the most useful way to organize the data? A table? A list? A diagram?

After the data are organized, have students check the data for common errors. Ask students to check the following items:

- Are there any transcription errors, where all students do not agree on what the correct data are?
- Has handwriting been interpreted correctly (e.g., no confusion of the characters 1/2/7/I/j, 0/8, 0/O)?
- Are all decimal points in the correct place (e.g., 0.1 vs. 0.01)? Are percentages correctly represented?
- Are any digits transposed (e.g., 0.72 vs. 0.27)?
- Are units reported correctly (e.g., cm vs. mm)?
- Does the range of values make sense (e.g., no insect body lengths below 0 cm and above 100 cm)?
- Are there any other transcription errors? Are all entries double-checked?
- Are there any missing data?

If errors are discovered, ask students to discuss the pros and cons of whether they should collect additional or replacement data, proceed after removing the erroneous data, or try to correct the data they do have. Key points to consider include time and resources, as well as the potential impact on the analyses. "Outlier" data points (very different from the rest) should be removed only if there is a clear rationale (e.g., student mistake while measuring) beyond dislike for the data point.

Grade-Level Differentiation

Elementary (3–5)

Collect notebooks after data collection to avoid data being lost or destroyed. Providing additional structure for data entry (Appendix 1) can be useful.

Middle (6–8)

Spreadsheet/computer use is more feasible.

High (9–12)

As noted earlier.

Examples

Figure 9.11 Preventing rain damage to datasheets using an umbrella and box clipboard

Collecting Data Outside

Figure 9.12 Teacher copying data to a whiteboard for sharing among students, then providing guidance on data analysis

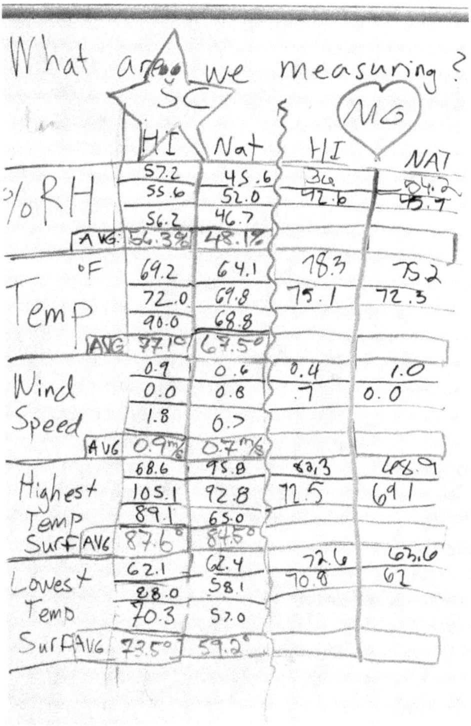

Figure 9.13 Combining multiple students' individual notes into a team dataset (middle school)

Figure 9.14 Calculating biodiversity metrics from data for later analysis (high school)

Figure 9.15 Entering data into a spreadsheet as backup and for computer graphing

Collecting Data Outside

This is a scatter plot of diversity and the percent of sand in the soil. Each dot is a single site.

Does diversity increase, decrease, or stay the same as the soil gets more sandy?

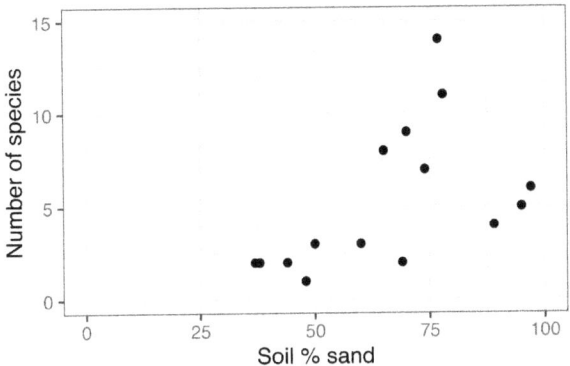

Figure 9.16 Teacher-generated graph of student data to support later analysis (middle school)

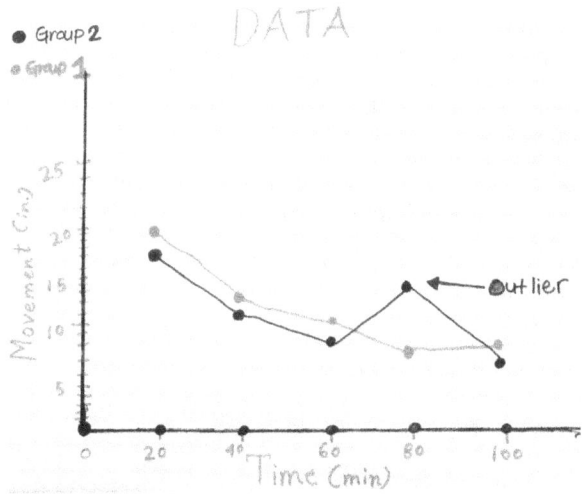

Figure 9.17 A dataset with an outlier point that students decided to not remove

10 Analyzing and Sense-Making

10.1 Drawing Conclusions from Data

Concepts

For descriptive projects, a conclusion can be made directly from the data (or visualization). Description is a process that reduces the complexity of the natural world into a dataset and, from there, reduces those data into a simpler summary. Description, therefore, loses information but gains interpretability.

Description helps students understand the world as it is (rather than how they may have thought it was), which is critical when intuition may be absent or misleading. Description also helps students build their relationship to place—both because they have now taken an action and found out something new about their home and also because descriptive data are always local and may reflect a reality different from similar phenomena in other places read about in textbooks.

Descriptive summaries of data can be quantitative and include summary statistics (e.g., mean + standard deviation + range) or graphs (e.g., bar plots, scatter plots). Summaries can also include narration (e.g., written, oral), collage (e.g., photo boards, edited video/audio, grouped sets of physical objects), or use other qualitative methods. Encouraging students to explore a variety of modalities to describe and summarize their findings will support a more intuitive understanding not only of the subject of the exploration but of mathematical concepts and presentation methods.

For hypothesis-driven projects, the process of making conclusions uses strong inference (Chapter 7) and the anchor chart (Appendix 1): your data either match or do not match each of the predefined predictions. Any hypotheses whose predictions do not match the data are rejected. If the hypotheses and predictions were set up as both contradictory to each other and covering all possible outcomes, some will always be rejected. You can then accept the hypothesis remaining as the correct answer. If multiple hypotheses remain (i.e., are not rejected), they are all potentially true answers, and the current study is insufficient to distinguish between them. Rejecting any hypotheses that did not correctly predict what the data would look like is a useful way to reduce the human tendency toward prejudice.

It can be unintuitive that positive conclusions can only be made by negative actions (rejecting alternative hypotheses). However, this is one of the most valuable learning outcomes: supporting a conclusion can only be done by first demonstrating that alternative explanations are wrong. This, in turn, requires listening to the data, whatever they may show.

Making an inference (coming to a conclusion) requires comparing the data to the predictions of the hypotheses. Recall that "prediction" does not mean "best guess"; instead it means "what would have to happen if the hypothesis were true." Recall also that you need to have at least two contradictory predictions for this process to work. In school projects, this comparison is primarily done via graphical interpretation. You draw a graph representing some feature(s) of the data and visually compare this graph to your verbal or graphical predictions on the anchor chart. Graphs that do not match a hypothesis's prediction reject that hypothesis. Graphing data is a valuable skill; the procedure trains students to interpret data in ways that allow them to arrive at conclusions by continuing the reduction process from reality to data to interpretation.

Data are never a perfect representation of reality. Measurements will always deviate by varying amounts. These deviations are usually not errors; rather, every measurement is affected by many factors (e.g., rock temperature affected by sunlight and wind speed). There is no hope of knowing or measuring all of the factors that influence the focal measurements. Instead, you can estimate the overall tendency in the data via repeated measurements. In this approach you let all of the factors vary randomly except for the one focal factor (e.g., measuring air temperature repeatedly, in sun and shade), then average out the effects of the unmeasured factors.

However, even when summarizing repeated measurements, the summaries may be subject to fluctuations based on variations in individual measurements. Inferential statistics, or "statistical tests," are tools that allow you to determine the level of uncertainty or confidence that is associated with any interpretation of averages (or other summaries of data). They give you quantitative ways to determine whether or not two graphs match and to determine your confidence in whether the data reject a given hypothesis (see Section 10.3). You may not arrive at a clear conclusion, or you may conclude something with limited confidence. This is a feature of reality and a key learning outcome for students.

Uncertainty in conclusions can also come from hypotheses and predictions that do not cover all possibilities. If all, or not enough, of your hypotheses have been rejected, then other hypotheses should have been considered. Or a different method for hypothesis testing (i.e., making additional predictions about other variables) should have been used. Careful study design can make such outcomes unlikely, but in practice, it does not prevent them altogether. If additional hypotheses are proposed in hindsight (perhaps due to new observations made during the study), these should be seen as important exploratory insights, even if they have not yet been tested by the study.

Data are necessarily place-based. This is both a strength and a weakness: they answer a question in one place and time, in a way that science done elsewhere cannot, but the answer cannot easily be generalized. Generalization only comes from many studies performed in many situations, and thus from weighing the evidence from each individual study against existing knowledge and other similar studies. Embracing the limits and specificity of knowledge is a better approach than excessive generalization.

Equity and Inclusion

For data that arise from the direct human experience of the world, there may always be aspects that cannot be simplified or summarized (e.g., the feeling of meeting an animal for the first time). Be careful to also value the work of students whose identities place a higher value on direct human experience than numbers, and make space for conclusions and presentations that support this type of description.

Implementation

For descriptive projects, encourage students to describe any discoveries they made both qualitatively and quantitatively. Qualitative descriptions may include observations of new animals or plants or behaviors, or other phenomena, like interactions between weather and animal behavior. Many qualitative observations can lead to new questions or new hypotheses for later projects and represent an important step for scientific discovery. Quantitative descriptions may include tables or graphs.

Both quantitative and qualitative descriptions are informative. If the question is "How many ants visit the schoolyard?," a good descriptive answer might be "More than we could count, and we also found some spiders we did not know about," or "Approximately 300 ants each day."

For hypothesis-driven projects, have students refamiliarize themselves with their anchor chart. As noted earlier, the chart should identify the necessary graph types already, so students should be able to make them. You may want to divide students into subgroups to make different graphs.

After undertaking this process, have students discuss which hypotheses are unlikely given the data and need to be rejected and which are not. The outcome of this discussion is the conclusion.

Students may be tempted to argue for a particular hypothesis or answer for reasons beyond the data. Limit discussion to what the data themselves indicate. You can ask students, "Is that idea supported by your data, or is it your opinion?" Opinions and speculation are also valuable but are better integrated at the reflection stage. Focus first on the facts; then you can expand to your opinions about these facts.

Grade-Level Differentiation

Elementary (3–5)

Use simpler graph types that use observations as directly as possible, with little intervening calculations. Skip statistical tests. It is reasonable to reject hypotheses based on the visual interpretation of graphs. The concept of quantifying uncertainty will be difficult. But understanding measurement variability (even for "the same thing") is important and possible

Analyzing and Sense-Making

with repeated direct experience and illustration of such variability (e.g., graphing all measurements and not only graphing averages).

Middle (6–8)

More complex graphs and relationships between measurements can be used. Skip statistical tests. Include variation as well as statistical summaries in graphs (e.g., a box-and-whisker plot in addition to plotting individual measurements).

High (9–12)

Consider introducing statistical tests. The results of students' projects may or may not agree with what a textbook says about the same question. You can discuss such discrepancies, but do not automatically dismiss the students' result as wrong: their results just may not generalize broadly.

Examples

Figure 10.1 Concluding that a hypothesis is supported (a study of insect diversity, fourth grade)

Analyzing and Sense-Making

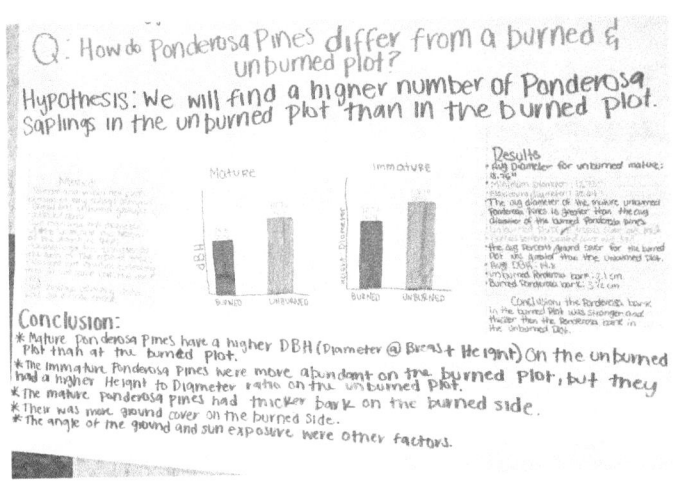

Figure 10.2 Concluding that a hypothesis is rejected but other descriptive findings were interesting (a study of fire impacts on forests)

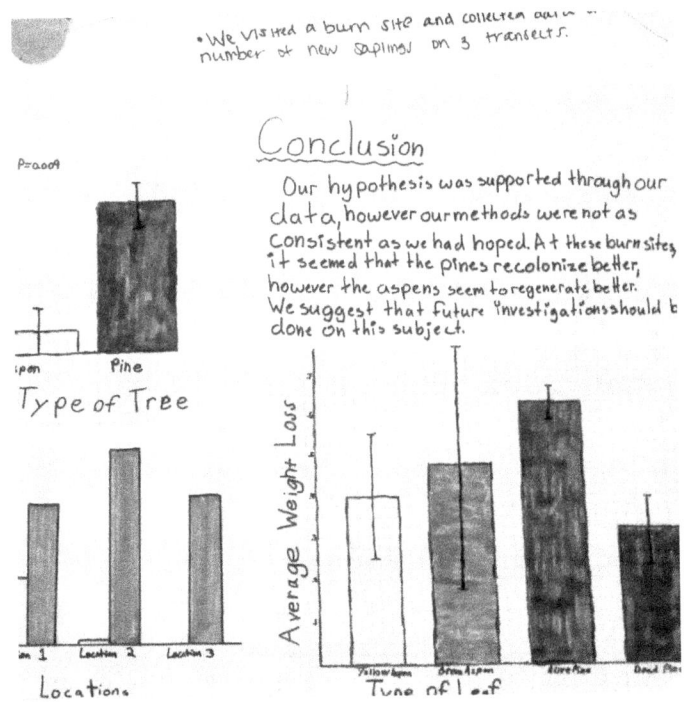

Figure 10.3 Concluding that a hypothesis is supported but confidence is limited (a study of tree regeneration)

203

Analyzing and Sense-Making

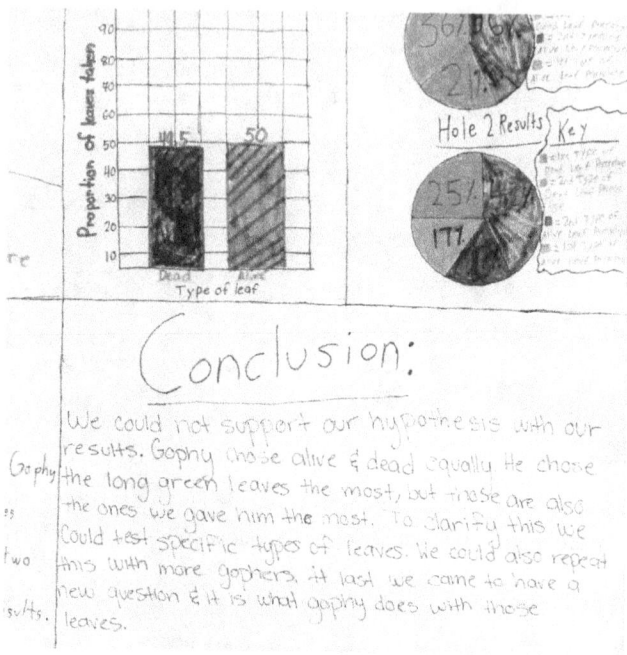

Figure 10.4 Concluding that a hypothesis is rejected (a study of gopher dietary preferences)

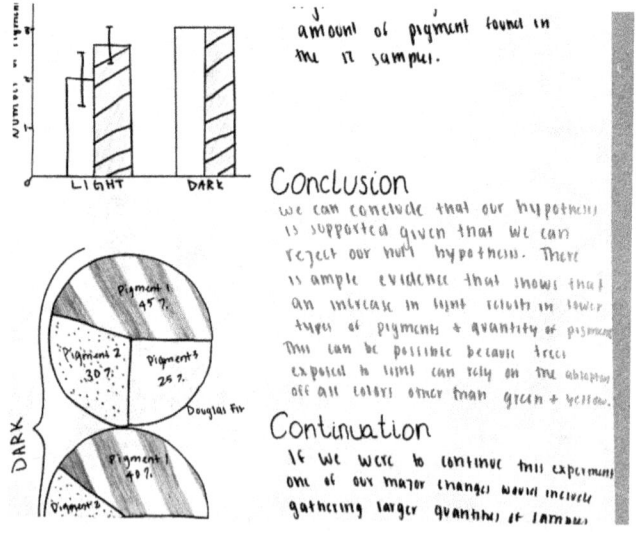

Figure 10.5 Concluding a hypothesis is supported (a study of plant pigmentation)

10.2 Visually Interpreting Results

Concepts

Graphing data makes numbers easier to interpret. Graphing each measurement as a data point visualizes the range of variation in the data and the amount of overlap between groups of measurements. This information helps determine your level of confidence in a conclusion.

Descriptive statistics can be used to make graphs summarizing data via averages, medians, standard deviations (a measure of variation), or other metrics. They are useful but always represent a loss of information. If you do not have a large number of values, you may be better off just focusing on visually interpreting the original numbers instead. In a descriptive project, interpretation of the graph is sufficient to come to a conclusion.

In a hypothesis-driven project, you are comparing the measurements against at least two qualitatively different, previously formulated possibilities. You will also already have decided on a graph type in your study design (Chapter 7). You can interpret each graph by deciding whether it "looks different from prediction A" (rejects the hypothesis), "looks like prediction A" (does not reject the hypothesis), or you are "not sure" (unclear conclusion) (see Section 10.2). There is no exact rule for making this decision, though statistical tests (see Section 10.3) can help. Interpreting available evidence always requires human judgment.

Do not be afraid of concluding that you are not sure; this is likely with small numbers of measurements. Using statistical tests will give you a clear decision criterion but still often lead to the same conclusion that there is not sufficient information to reject a hypothesis. In these cases, either more data or a different study are needed to answer the question.

Equity and Inclusion

Students who are colorblind may not be able to interpret graphs that differentiate data with certain colors. Encourage students to use alternate color pairings, even if you are not aware of any colorblind students, to support sharing data with broader communities. Replacing red-green palettes with blue-yellow palettes will help the majority of people.

Analyzing and Sense-Making

Students who are visually impaired may have difficulty creating or interpreting graphs on paper or on the computer. Students also can interpret data tactually as well as visually. If using paper, consider making graphs that have raised surfaces to indicate axes and data points (e.g., corkboard with pinned-on cardboard, buttons, pipe cleaners, or 3D-printed surfaces). Accessible graphs also can be created using tactile graph sheets/kits or graphic aids (Maguvhe, 2015; Moon et al., 2012). Both are commercially available.

When sharing computer graphs, visual elements should also be alt-tagged with appropriate text descriptions. If using computers, ensure students have access to screen reader software. Additionally, consider obtaining access to data sonification programs that convert numbers and graphs to sounds or music and permit audio interpretation of data. Free options for both can be found via an Internet search.

Implementation

Consider having students draw graphs on paper by hand. Doing so gives students—especially at younger grade levels—the chance to grapple with numbers and all the parts of a graph and to practice numerical and algebraic skills in manipulating numbers. Drawing graphs by hand also provides extra opportunities to practice fine motor skills and mark out measured intervals on axes. Letting each student add their measurements to a group graph can help engage everyone in the graphing process. Some graphs will take a few iterations to get right.

Alternatively, you can use computers and other digital tools to assist with graphing. Computer graphs free up student time to think about other aspects of the project and build digital literacy. However, if less than one computer or device per student is available, making graphs by hand may enable more students to engage with the process. If you decide to have students share a computer to make graphs, try to assign different graphs or parts of the analysis to different students, or encourage a process where one student types or uses the mouse and another student directs, to enable all students to actively engage and contribute to the software use. Spreadsheet software can generate bar plots and scatter plots; however, it is harder to find software that produces box plots or strip plots. More advanced free graphing programs can be found via an Internet search.

Analyzing and Sense-Making

Grade-Level Differentiation

Elementary (3–5)

Strip plots or bar plots are most intuitive. You may have to help students translate measurements to positions on graph axes. If you can, introduce the same graph type on smaller datasets before embarking on a longer inquiry project (e.g., small surveys in the classroom, such as, "What is your favorite ice cream flavor?"). You can also prepare a blank graph for students to add data/labels to.

Middle (6–8)

Two-dimensional scatter plots can be used. Summary statistics can be introduced, allowing you to graph in box plots; individual measurements also can be graphed on such plots. Pie plots can be used to practice fractions.

High (9–12)

Highlight variation in measurements (e.g., by including all data points in a strip plot or by using a box plot). If you are also including statistical tests (see Section 10.3), encourage discussion about the pros and cons of each approach.

Examples

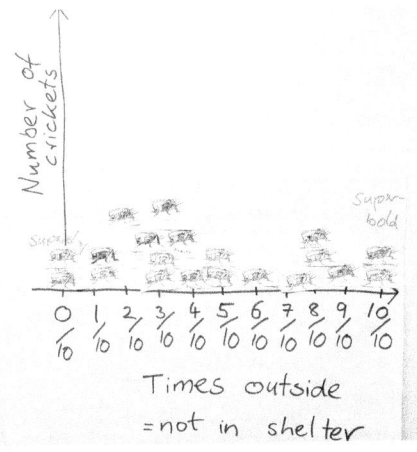

Figure 10.6 Visually interpreting a frequency plot to conclude that cricket behavior does vary among individuals; see Figure 7.8

Analyzing and Sense-Making

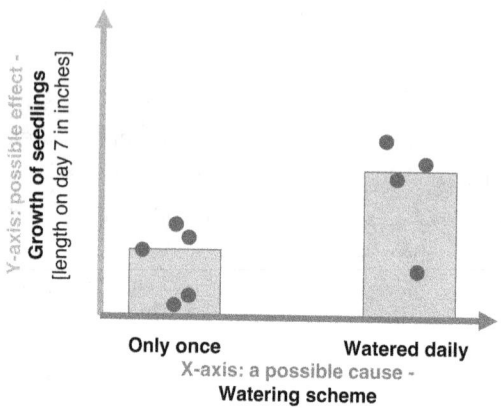

Figure 10.7 Visually inspecting a strip plot/bar plot with medians to conclude that watering does increase seedling growth; see Figure 7.7

Plant height variation: Elementary students wanted to know why plants in their schoolyard varied in height and tested the hypotheses that "Plants grow better with regular water availability" and "Water availability plays no role in plant growth." The students used a randomized controlled trial study design. Ten seeds from a schoolyard plant were placed in ten small pots and either watered once at the beginning of the study or every day for a week. On Day 7, students measured the length of seedlings with a ruler. One pot was accidentally destroyed. The students graphed "Watering scheme" (X) and "Growth of seedlings" (Y). They graphed each data point (seedling) as well as the median (bar height). The median for the daily watered plants is much higher, but the spread of the data points overlaps. They could potentially reject the hypothesis that watering plays no role (based on the higher median), but also admit that there is substantial uncertainty in this conclusion.

Fuchsia flowers: Middle school students were curious about the showy flowers on California fuchsia bushes growing in their schoolyard. They tested the hypotheses that (1) more sunlight would lead to more reproduction through more investment in flower parts and (2) that the response would be stronger for female flowers because their eventual fruits are dispersed better if they are visible. They selected male and female flowers in sites with differing light intensities, then measured flower part masses using a cross-sectional study design. They graphed flower mass (Y) and light level (X), coloring data by flower sex, on a scatter plot. They concluded that the female part of the flower (carpel) was heavier but also that it responded more to increased

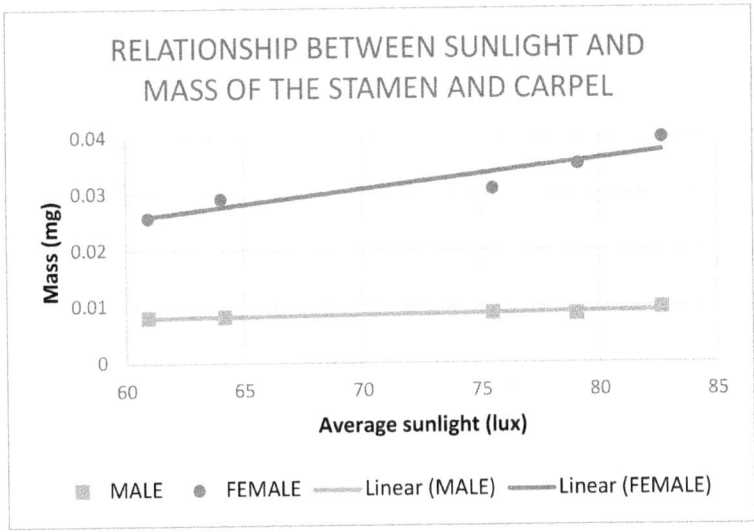

Figure 10.8 Visually interpreting a scatter plot to support the hypotheses that flower mass increases with sunlight and that females respond more strongly than males

sunlight (steeper slope of the line) than the male part of the flower (stamen). Because the data are close to the line, it is unlikely that there is truly no relationship between the X and Y variables. The students concluded that both hypotheses were supported, compared to the implicit alternatives that sunlight did not affect investment in flower parts or that both sexes would respond equally.

Fire effects: High school students investigated the effects of fire on different species of trees in Arizona's Catalina Mountains. They first performed a descriptive study, counting the number of trees of different species in a defined area of burned and unburned areas. Using a pie plot, they discovered that primarily ponderosa pine and Douglas fir seemed to have survived in burned areas. The students then asked two separate questions, using a cross-sectional study design, where they visited burned and unburned areas and measured tree properties in each. First, they asked if the thickness of bark would determine whether trees can survive a forest fire, hypothesizing that thicker bark would help (with the alternative that it would not, because other traits determine fire survival). This led to the predictions that ponderosa pine and Douglas fir would have thicker bark than other trees (or not). Measuring bark thickness for all

Analyzing and Sense-Making

species in the unburned area and plotting it on a bar plot (average bark thickness [Y] and species [X]), they found taller bars for the two species that survived best in burned areas. However, one other species (aspen) also had relatively thick bark. The students concluded that there was support for the first hypothesis, but they could not accept it with high confidence. Second, they asked whether bigger trees might be able to better survive forest fires. They hypothesized that trees in burnt areas should have larger sizes, or alternatively, that they would not because other traits determine fire survival. They measured circumference for individual trees of the two focal species that survived best in the burned area. They plotted tree circumference (Y) and area (X) using a box plot. Using visual interpretation, they found trees actually were bigger in unburned areas. They therefore rejected the first hypothesis with high confidence. They speculated about fire recovery as an alternative explanation.

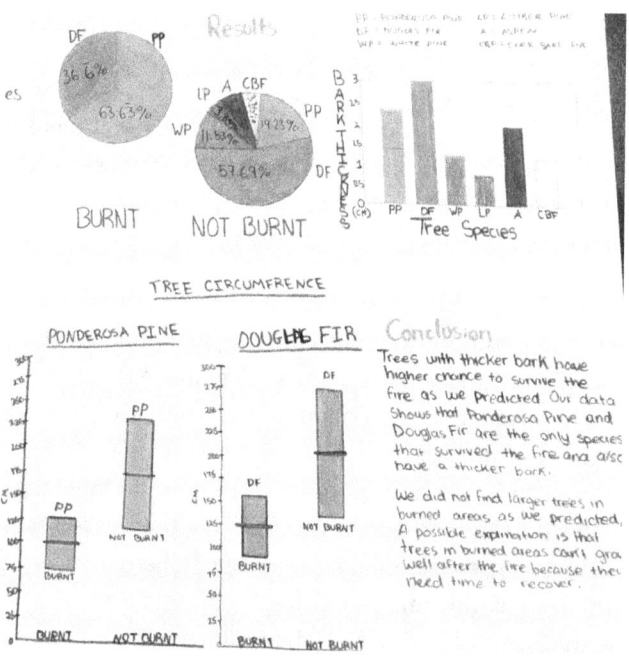

Figure 10.9 Describing variation in forest composition (top left), visually interpreting bar plots to support a hypothesis about bark thickness among species (top right), and visually interpreting box plots to reject a hypothesis about fire impacts on size (bottom)

Analyzing and Sense-Making

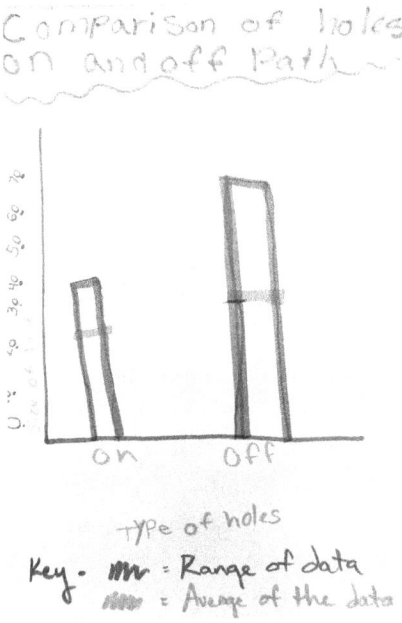

Figure 10.10 Visual interpretation yields an unclear conclusion about animal hole size on and off a path (averages are similar but ranges are large)

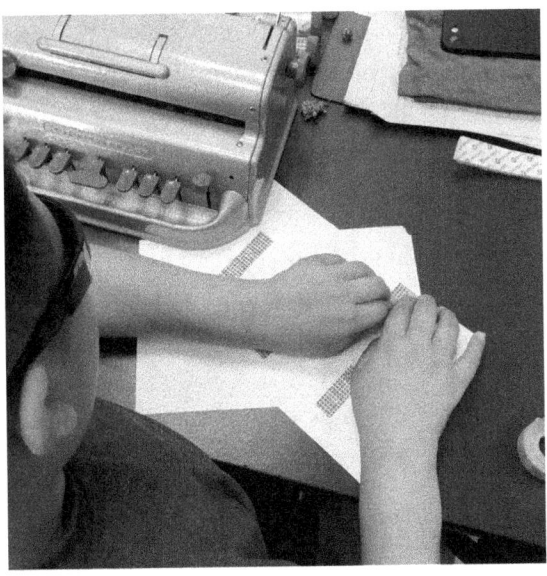

Figure 10.11 Tactile interpretation of a bar plot using sticky tape for data and embossing (from a braille machine) for axes

10.3 Statistical Tests

Concepts

If you want to go further in the analysis of your results than visual interpretation allows, you can introduce students to inferential statistics. Inferential statistics help to compare data to predictions by quantifying the uncertainty associated with different conclusions. This process formalizes the graph interpretation process by giving objective criteria for determining when a hypothesis should be rejected.

In a statistical test, you declare a default or "null" hypothesis and decide that you will accept this null hypothesis in all cases except when there is strong evidence against it. Most tests calculate a p-value, which is the probability that the measurements look as they did (or more extreme) if the null hypothesis is true. Standard practice is to accept the null hypothesis unless $p < 5\%$ (i.e., $p < 0.05$); in other words, you want to ensure that you have no more than a 5% chance of error of accepting the alternative hypothesis when this is in fact not true (i.e., you want no more than a 5% chance of false-positive errors; see the table below).

A t-test or analysis of variance (ANOVA) can be used to compare the difference in measurements between groups. These tests calculate a p-value for the null hypothesis that the difference between the means of two groups is zero (t-test) or that the difference in means among three or more groups is zero (ANOVA). A linear regression can be used to determine if a relationship between two continuous variables exists or not. Regressions estimate a line of best fit (with a slope and intercept). They typically calculate a p-value for a null hypothesis that there is no relationship (the slope is zero).

The real world →	Null hypothesis actually true	Null hypothesis actually not true
Your conclusion ↓		
Null hypothesis accepted, alternative rejected because p > 0.05	Correct inference	*False negative*: you incorrectly failed to reject the null hypothesis, perhaps because of low sample size or high variation in measurements. The probability of this error is hard to estimate and can be high.
Null hypothesis rejected, alternative accepted because p < 0.05	*False positive*: you incorrectly rejected the null hypothesis. The probability of this error is, by assumption, 5% out of all cases where the null hypothesis actually is true.	Correct inference

These tests do not tell you how likely it is that the null hypothesis, or any other hypothesis, is true. "Accepting the null hypothesis" here means simply that you act as if the null hypothesis is true and the alternative hypothesis is false; you may realize that there is considerable uncertainty associated with this inference but consider the available evidence insufficient to accept the alternative hypothesis.

No test or dataset is perfect, and statistical error may occur. Different error types are shown in the above table. In a real study, you only know your conclusion (whether you are in the first or second row); you do not know whether or not you are making an error (whether you are in the first or second column). In any decision, changing your decision strategy can only decrease one error type by increasing the other (e.g., decrease the probability of false positives by increasing the probability of false negatives, or vice versa). However, increasing the sample size (number of measurements) is a straightforward way to reduce the chance of false negatives.

You should also consider not only whether something happens but how often or how large its effect is. It only makes sense to talk about effect size if you are reasonably convinced that there is an effect (i.e., you have visually or statistically concluded that the treatments are different). For comparison between categories (e.g., bar or strip plots with t-tests), the difference in means (height of bars) is often used as a metric of effect size. For continuous variables (e.g., a scatter plot with a linear regression), the R^2 metric is commonly used.

Statistical tests are often misunderstood. You can skip statistical tests unless you feel comfortable with the arguments presented earlier. If you do not have a lot of data, applying statistical tests may not add much insight for students and may make the conclusions harder to understand.

Equity and Inclusion

Consider access if you are asking students to produce graphs on a computer. You should not ask students to complete complex or novel tasks outside of school time. You cannot assume either the ready availability of computing devices or Internet access in all students' homes. Computing tasks are best performed at school, on devices that have been provided, and where you can ensure that each student or small group gets an equitable share of time to use available devices.

Implementation

If students have access to a computer, spreadsheet software will allow simple graphing of data and basic statistical tests. Alternatively, if you have Internet access, many websites carry out these tests directly after you type or paste in data (e.g., search for t-test calculator).

Grade-Level Differentiation

Elementary (3–5)

Focus on visual interpretation of results. Descriptive statistics can be introduced.

Middle (6–8)

Confidence and error types/consequences can be introduced. Visual interpretation of results is still preferred.

High (9–12)

Statistical tests can be introduced.

Examples

Plant height variation: In Figure 10.2, the null hypothesis could be that watering does not affect plant growth, meaning that the two treatments (watered vs. not watered) should have similar measurements. A t-test applied to these data shows that the probability of getting an observed difference in means as big or bigger if the null hypothesis were true is $p = 8\%$. Thus, the null hypothesis (that there is no difference in plant growth between the watered and unwatered treatments) would not be rejected (because $p > 5\%$). Even though the observed data may appear to differ among treatments, the t-test indicates that you cannot be sure that there was an effect of treatment.

Cactus spines: Barrel cacti are common in the Sonoran Desert. They have clusters of spines on all sides that shield them from herbivores and also shade their photosynthetic surfaces. Students were curious about whether cacti grew spines at different densities depending on sun intensity and shading. They used a cross-sectional study design. They selected several cacti, measured the amount of shade they experienced during a day, and also measured the number of spine clusters. They made a scatter plot (X, number of spine clusters; Y, % shade). They used a statistics program to do a linear regression, which calculated that $p = 0.08$, $R^2 = 0.19$, and $y = 0.04x + 8.8$. Finding $p > 0.05$ means that they cannot reject the null hypothesis, namely that the number of spine clusters does not change with the amount of shade. Even if the p-value were smaller, the factor 0.04 before x indicates that the slope of the regression line is low, that is, the best estimate would be that only one spine cluster is added for every 25% more shade ($1 = 0.04 \times 25$). The R^2 value is also somewhat low, indicating that if shade affects spine clusters at all, it only explains about 19% of the variation in spine cluster number.

Analyzing and Sense-Making

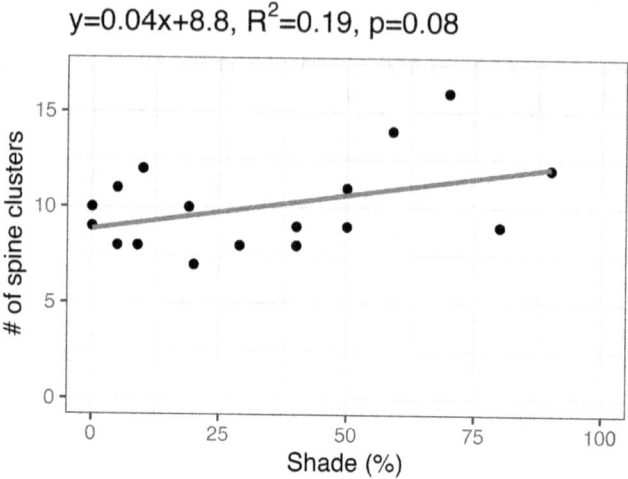

Figure 10.12 Failing to reject a hypothesis that spine cluster counts and shade level are not associated, using linear regression, even though the slope appears positive - i.e., the conclusion is no effect of shade

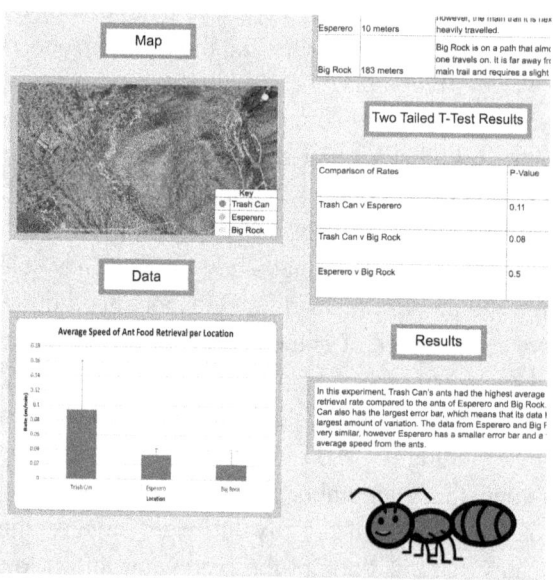

Figure 10.13 Failing to reject a hypothesis that ant food retrieval speed is the same among site pairs, using t-tests, even though the group medians appear to differ. An ANOVA could also be used. Thus the conclusion is that retrieval speed is the same across sites

Analyzing and Sense-Making

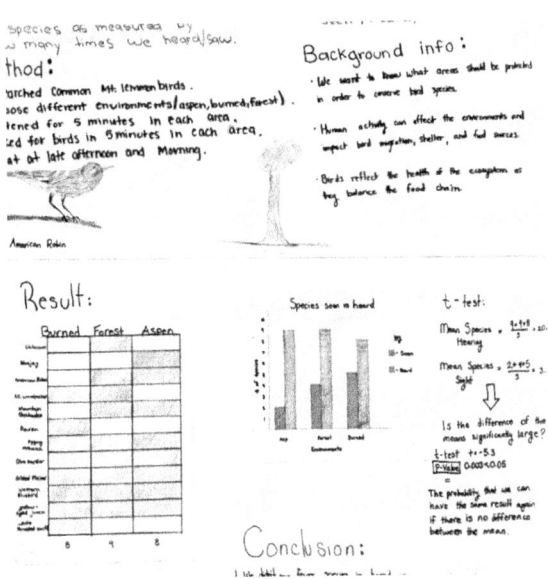

Figure 10.14 Rejecting the hypothesis that there is no difference in the number of bird species seen or heard in the forest, using a t-test (bottom right); thus concluding that there is a difference in bird species seen and heard

# Reflecting and Recognizing Success

11.1 Reflection

Concepts

Each project contributes toward broader knowledge and sits within broader societal values and structures. After completing their projects, students should reflect on their findings and consider the relevance to their places, communities, and futures. Additionally, students should develop explanations for their results that enable sense-making and connection to broader scientific ideas (Braaten & Windschitl, 2011).

Reflection around findings is important. Findings should be connected to the Disciplinary Core Ideas and Crosscutting Concepts relevant to the overall curriculum (Schwarz et al., 2017; Windschitl et al., 2018). Students should explain their findings and contextualize them relative to their current knowledge, helping them connect their projects to classroom learning. What students discover may be surprising, interesting, or challenging to prior beliefs/knowledge, thus helping them develop their identity as learners and scientists.

Reflection around the scientific inquiry process is important. Findings should be connected to the Science and Engineering Practices to help students explicitly recognize the skills they are developing and the tools that they are using to answer their questions (e.g., engaging in argument from evidence). Process reflection helps students recognize how many subjective decisions they had to make in the design/implementation of their project and how hard it is to obtain trustworthy data.

Reflection around identity and peers is important. Students can come to see themselves or their peers in new ways. They can celebrate how they have worked collaboratively, learned new things about each other, and handled conflict when it arose.

Reflection around place relationships is important. Students can come to see familiar places in new ways and gain greater humility and empathy for the communities of people and organisms that use these places. Students may have discovered the uniqueness and value of their place for the first time and be able to contrast this perspective with potentially negative ones they were exposed to by other people, in books, and in media.

Reflection around justice is also important. Students can synthesize the conclusions they have made, and the place connections they have experienced, to consider whether these connections are fair and how these connections might change. They can also reflect on their own roles and responsibilities in the community and the place.

Equity and Inclusion

Reflection is a key time to encourage students to think critically about place relationships and decolonization. You can open conversations around why you and your students were able to do their projects in the place and who should inhabit or take care of this land (if not the current inhabitants). You can also discuss what it means to own land and what the differences are between owning, renting, and caring for land (Kimmerer, 2013; Zinn, 2015). Holding these conversations requires you to have some level of background knowledge (e.g., readings like the references provided in Chapter 2).

Implementation

Allow students to reflect individually, then share one by one in a team setting. Students may come to different reflections. You can have students write thoughts down first, and then allow each student to share to avoid having responses dominated by whoever speaks first; or have all students write something on the whiteboard (more or less simultaneously), and then review what is written there as a group. Enumerating all reflections and then allowing students time to discuss is a fairer process and produces a broader set of thoughtful points.

The following questions can be used to structure reflection. Some questions focus on subjective experiences, and others can be used to support students in aligning their thinking to Next Generation Science Standards (NGSS) principles.

Reflection around findings:

- Which hypotheses were not rejected by your data?
- What evidence did you use to make your conclusions?
- How confident are you in your conclusions?
- How do your findings support or challenge what you know about [Disciplinary Core Idea X]?
- What did you change your mind about based on your project?
- Did your project demonstrate cause and effect?
- Would your conclusion potentially change at a different spatial/biological/physical scale?
- Do your findings reflect stability or change in the natural world? How?

Reflection around process:

- How did you use [Science and Engineering Practice X] in your project?
- What was surprising to you about doing [Science and Engineering Practice X] while working on your project?
- What could you do to increase confidence in your findings?
- What could you have done differently, and why could it have made the project better?
- If you had more money or time, what else would you want to find out?

Reflection around self/peers:

- Who helped the team to succeed? Who surprised you and how?
- What was one way that you helped the project?
- Could you have done the project alone?
- What did you learn about working in a group?

Reflection around place relationships:

- Are your findings specific to this place, or where do they generalize to?
- Do you now understand this place differently? How?
- Could your results help others understand this place differently?
- Who in your community would care about the findings from your project?
- What would you tell your family about why your project matters?

Reflection around justice:

- What do you think should change about this place?
- What would make this place fairer or better?
- What should your school/city/neighbors do differently based on your results?
- Who should own or care for this place?

Reflection provides an opportunity to use student responses to recognize student success, plan further inquiry projects, or develop community or activism-focused work.

Grade-Level Differentiation

Elementary (3–5)

Reflection can become too abstract and removed from the action or event you are reflecting on. It may be more useful to insert short reflection sessions throughout the inquiry project and its presentation to others. It may be most effective to pick one of the Crosscutting Concepts to focus on throughout the project and to reconnect student thinking to this concept repeatedly and at the end. For example, you can integrate discussions of scale throughout, from planning and executing measurements, to graphing axes and effect sizes; in the reflection phase, you may then encourage students to discuss how changing the scale of measurements or the scale of effects would have changed the project and its outcomes.

Reflecting and Recognizing Success

Middle (6–8)

Students are able to start reflecting on the overall project and the impact of their own actions and the scientific process. Encourage discussion on your preferred aspect of reflection and direct their attention to the role of Crosscutting Concepts in this topic. For example, if you choose to focus on place relationships, you can connect these to systems thinking by discussing the multiple ways in which humans, landscapes, and ecosystems interact and how this was reflected in your specific project(s).

High (9–12)

You can spend more time on reflection and include more self-awareness (i.e., reflection around process, relationships, and justice). You may also be able to include more actions as a result (e.g., follow-up projects or activism). Students may be able to reflect more deeply and independently on several Crosscutting Concepts and their role in the execution and interpretation of their project.

Examples

Figure 11.1 Sitting outside in a large circle supports sharing reflections

11.2 Recognition

Concepts

Recognition of success and growth helps to close out a project. Recognition helps reinforce the idea that science is conducted in a community of people who participate in and gain from the process in different, and often complementary, ways. Recognition also helps students understand how their success has been supported by the place they studied, further building place relationships.

Equity and Inclusion

Set the expectation that every student gets recognized at least once. Implicit student biases may otherwise cause peers in marginalized groups to be less likely to receive positive feedback. Avoid structures that can let some students get skipped.

Implementation

Recognizing success can follow, or be integrated with, reflection. It differs by focusing on celebration. Within small groups, have each student identify:

- What do you want to recognize about the student next to you?
- What is one thing someone else did that contributed positively to the overall team (teammates, community members, the place itself)? What was the contribution? How did they do it?
- What new knowledge or perspective have you or someone else gained?
- What roles were you able to take during the project?
- Has the team met its goals?
- Has the team been accountable to the peer expectations set out at the beginning of the project?

Reflecting and Recognizing Success

- Was the team respectful to the community and place?
- What did you get better at throughout the project?

You can also have students synthesize their experience by asking them to share:

- The most surprising thing they learned?
- Their favorite experience?
- Something new they learned about another student?
- A positive thing they want to recognize in another student?
- An act of kindness they witnessed?
- What they will share with their family?

Recognitions can be shared within small groups. In circles, students can go in order or "popcorn"—each student shares, then chooses another student—until everyone has been chosen. Alternatively students can make their recognitions individually (e.g., on paper plates that can be given as "awards" to peers, on sticky notes that can be put on a shared poster, or on a shared digital platform).

You can also share your own recognitions with students as long as you share equally with all groups and/or students. Consider answering one of the earlier questions for each group in a whole-group or whole-classroom setting.

Grade-Level Differentiation

Elementary (3–5)

Keep questions simpler and recognition time shorter. Structure the activity to ensure that it is focused on celebration (e.g., ask about their favorite part of the project). Students may benefit from receiving a physical object symbolizing their recognition.

Middle (6–8)

Students may worry about favoritism, so focus on celebration and do not give selective praise.

High (9–12)

Longer reflection and individually directed feedback are possible.

Examples

Figure 11.2 Students celebrating their successful project

# Sharing Outcomes

12.1 How and Why to Share Projects

Concepts

Sharing projects helps students recall and synthesize information, builds communication skills, and helps them feel that their efforts are valuable and recognized. Sharing also builds relationships between students, teachers, and the community. Sharing benefits the community by disseminating knowledge and generating or reinforcing a shared sense of place. Sharing can also benefit the place and the broader community by building awareness and calling for action.

Sharing typically occurs via student presentations, which may be individual, group, or whole-class products. Presentations are not only posters or slide presentations; any format that reaches its audience is appropriate. Depending on the interests and availability of the audience and the presenters, presentations can be short and include only major conclusions or implications of the project, or long, with a detailed report of how the inquiry project was performed.

Physical artifacts that relate to the project can enhance presentations. For example, a bar plot summarizing the number of leaves found in different places could be made of leaves glued onto paper. A team that studied rock hardness could bring some cracked-open rocks to pass out to peers. Students could create models or dioramas, possibly with natural materials. Similarly, recorded sounds or video (e.g., recorded via smartphone) could be used to share study sites, methods, or stories about team members.

DOI: 10.4324/9781003367192-12

This chapter has been made available under a CC-BY license.

Equity and Inclusion

Be mindful of what you expect students to accomplish when sharing their project outside the classroom, especially if it may involve special equipment (e.g., computers, phones), infrastructure (e.g., Internet access), or parent/guardian support (e.g., purchasing poster boards). Supplies, equipment, and infrastructure should be provided at school. Select modes of sharing that require minimal investment if resources are lacking at school.

Presenting at science fairs allows students to showcase their work widely. Place-based projects are not common at science fairs, so event organizers may not provide templates or entry categories that match your projects. You should still encourage students to present their work in their preferred format. You may need to contact organizers in advance. Like all events taking place outside of the school building and hours, reduce barriers (e.g., transportation costs) for students as much as possible and leave participation optional.

Implementation

Set clear expectations that sharing outcomes is a key part of the inquiry process. Decide (potentially with your students) who the projects should be shared with. At a minimum, projects should be shared with your classroom among multiple student teams. Sharing with the school community and parents should also be possible at low or no cost and will bring increased benefits for the students, yourself, and your community. It may also be possible to share with broader community members, or with landowners/rightsholders and other partners. You should also ask your students if there are particular groups of people they feel it would be important to share their projects with.

Decide with your students what format for sharing would be effective and logistically feasible for your selected audience. Using a diversity of presentation formats can provide students multiple ways of demonstrating their engagement with the learning process and also be more interesting for other students. Possible presentation modes include:

- Show-and-tell
- Letters to parents
- Hand-drawn poster/oral presentation

Sharing Outcomes

- Digital slide presentation/oral presentation
- Group video presentation
- Structured conversation
- Question/answer session
- Skit/drama
- Dance
- Visual art
- Zine
- Comic
- Signage
- Podcast
- Blog post
- Social media posts

Plan to archive the presentation in some way (e.g., by keeping physical artifacts or a video recording). You can share recordings later on and can give future access to students examples of past student work, to provide examples of high-quality projects that can be achieved

Grade-Level Differentiation

Elementary (3–5)

Integrate sharing throughout the project. Letters to parents/guardians and show-and-tell are effective. Simple posters summarizing methods and results are possible.

Middle (6–8)

Students can use more freedom to choose among presentation modes.

High (9–12)

If time allows, students can develop multiple forms of presentations targeted to different audiences and purposes.

Sharing Outcomes

Examples

Figure 12.1 Sharing poster presentations in the classroom

Figure 12.2 Dramatizing a project through a skit; here, a scientist (center) observing a squirrel (right) approaching a tree (left)

Sharing Outcomes

Figure 12.3 Drawing comics to show project methods

Figure 12.4 Sharing a project at a regional science fair

Sharing Outcomes

Figure 12.5 Recording video of student presentations for distribution to family

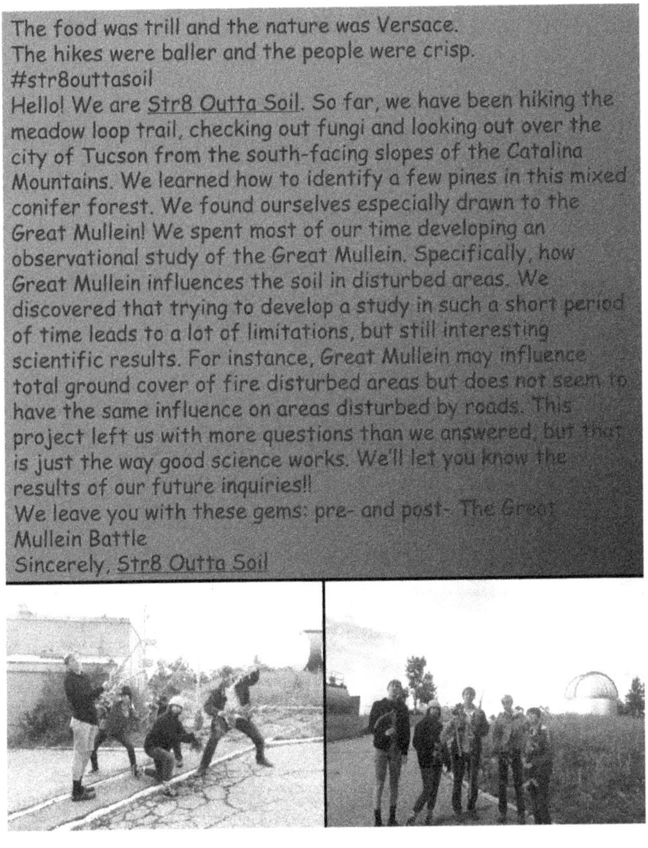

The food was trill and the nature was Versace.
The hikes were baller and the people were crisp.
#str8outtasoil
Hello! We are Str8 Outta Soil. So far, we have been hiking the meadow loop trail, checking out fungi and looking out over the city of Tucson from the south-facing slopes of the Catalina Mountains. We learned how to identify a few pines in this mixed conifer forest. We found ourselves especially drawn to the Great Mullein! We spent most of our time developing an observational study of the Great Mullein. Specifically, how Great Mullein influences the soil in disturbed areas. We discovered that trying to develop a study in such a short period of time leads to a lot of limitations, but still interesting scientific results. For instance, Great Mullein may influence total ground cover of fire disturbed areas but does not seem to have the same influence on areas disturbed by roads. This project left us with more questions than we answered, but that is just the way good science works. We'll let you know the results of our future inquiries!!
We leave you with these gems: pre- and post- The Great Mullein Battle
Sincerely, Str8 Outta Soil

Figure 12.6 Writing a blog post for Internet distribution

12.2 Supporting Presentation Development

Concepts

Making a presentation is like telling a story. A good story creates a connection with its audience; has a clear beginning, middle, and end; and creates a tension that is then resolved. That is, a good presentation is about emotion and place connection as much as it is about facts.

One way to tell a story is via an hourglass form. Hourglass presentations start "wide," drawing the audience in with the motivation for their inquiry: a pressing problem in the community, a notable observation, or a personal experience that motivated curiosity. The presentation "narrows" as it focuses on the students' particular experimental design: a specific inquiry question (and hypotheses if present), methods, and quantitative results. The presentation ends "wide" via a general conclusion based on strong inference, a reflection on the implications of their results for the place and the community, and/or their own personal growth.

You can modify this form or adopt others that are more culturally relevant to your students. For example, students may make an infographic to publish in a school newsletter, or they may audio-record each other's recollections to share with another classroom.

Equity and Inclusion

Presentations are a way for students to build further relationships with their projects, their team, and their place. Keep focus on the students as much as on the end product. All students should participate in some way in the presentation, though the modality of their contribution may vary within a team (e.g., one student may make art while another may speak). The method that is most accessible for a student to demonstrate understanding is the one that should be encouraged. You should help students feel valued and respected, not create uncertainty and anxiety.

Implementation

Start with the audience in mind. Ask students to visualize specific people as an audience (e.g., a friend in another classroom, a grandparent). Ask students to imagine that they are helping that person understand what their inquiry project was about. Thinking of specific people also helps maintain motivation at the end of the project. Ask students: What would you say to [this person] about why you were interested in this question? What different answers were you trying to decide between? What would [this person] find funny, or interesting, or relevant to their life about your project or results? How were you able to tell which answer was the right one? Who is affected by the answer, and who should care? Answering these questions via a brainstorming session similar to the question generation/winnowing process can be useful.

Once students have a story to tell and they have decided on a presentation mode, they can work together to assign individual responsibility for different components of the presentation. Components may include not only writing different sections, drawing illustrations, and preparing media or recording equipment, but also planning a live event, inviting an audience, or managing dissemination of the product. Be prepared for conflict and/or confusion to arise at this stage. Investing further time in team building can be helpful. You can also float between groups or require that teams check in with you to share their plan and foreseen obstacles before proceeding.

If possible, allocate time for iteration. Drafting and then improving work is often initially difficult for students. Explain to students that presentations should reflect their best work and that work can always be improved with feedback. Practicing presentations to peer groups can yield supportive and constructive feedback.

Provide a rubric and examples of what makes a good presentation (or, alternatively, what makes a bad presentation). This will allow students to understand the level of work and detail that is expected of their presentation, which is especially important if you are allowing students to freely choose a presentation mode. Some modes may require more effort than others; some may be more or less suitable for conveying key information. All presentations should be equally effective at engaging an audience and communicating the work that has been accomplished. Sample rubrics are provided in Appendix 3.

Posters or digital slideshows are valuable, especially if students are presenting at a science fair. In this case, having one student in charge of poster/slideshow layout while others take charge of writing text, drawing graphs, or making illustrations can be helpful. Plan to use more space and less text than you and your students originally think is needed. Consider using large illustrations and/or photos. Avoid large blocks of small text.

For physical posters, students should use pencils to sketch a layout before committing to markers, glue, or other permanent materials.

Grade-Level Differentiation

Elementary (3–5)

It is often difficult for students to imagine others not knowing what they know, making presentation development difficult. You can replace a final presentation with more frequent mini-reports throughout the project. Writing and drawing skills will also vary widely, so it is important to find a form of project/results sharing that plays to each student's strength. Consider simply allowing spontaneous storytelling (and recording via audio) or having students combine writing and drawing as they prefer.

Middle (6–8)

Students can plan their own presentations. Explaining conclusions based on data can be difficult, so you may want to have students practice their explanations with you first. Provide time for students to allocate roles for presentation development.

High (9–12)

As noted earlier.

Examples

Figure 12.7 Students dividing the work of poster development. The teacher (far right) does not need to actively support this well-functioning team

Sharing Outcomes

Figure 12.8 Peers provide input on a whiteboard draft of a poster

Figure 12.9 Natural objects (here, seeds) are included on a poster

235

Sharing Outcomes

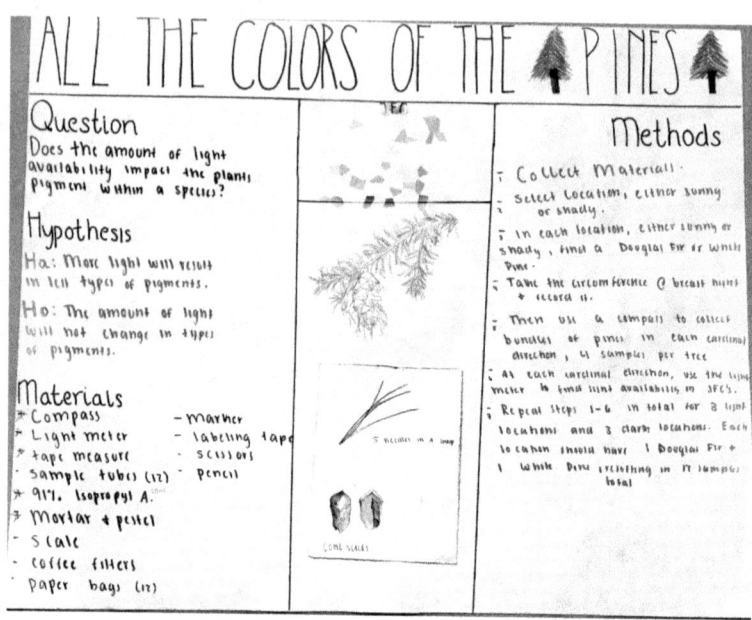

Figure 12.10 Detailed illustrations of plant anatomy provided by an artistically inclined student

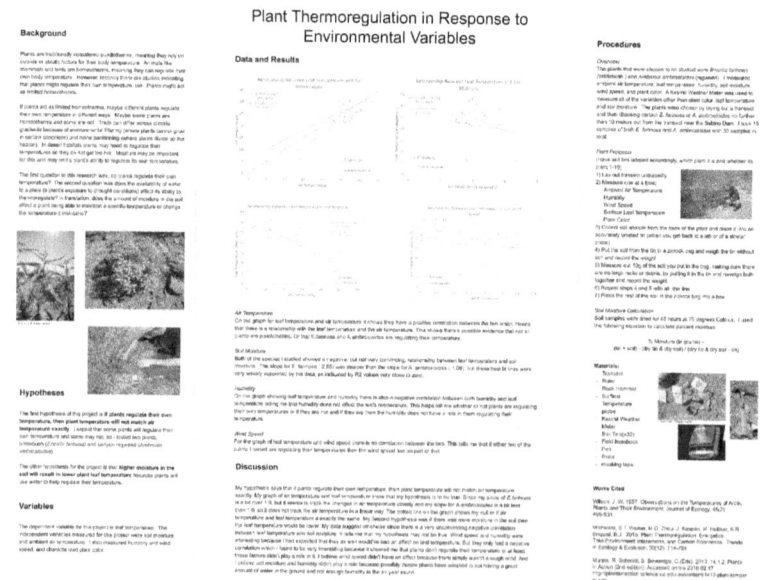

Figure 12.11 A digitally prepared presentation

Sharing Outcomes

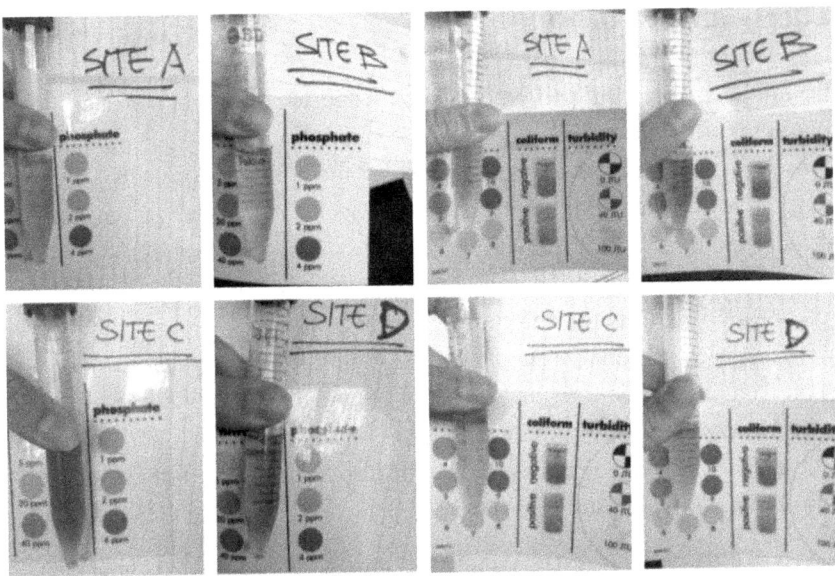

Figure 12.12 Photos of data collection steps for inclusion in a digital presentation

12.3 Holding a Community Event

Concepts

Holding a community event provides an opportunity for students to share their projects with a community. The community can be defined as narrowly as other students within the classroom, or more broadly to include other students at the school, school staff (e.g., administrative and janitorial staff, other teachers), community groups, city representatives, faith community leaders, or other landowners, rightsholders, and partners. People are part of the community if they are interested in your students or have a relationship to the focal place.

Community events celebrate the achievement of each project and each student, share knowledge and values, and provide a forum for encouraging future action or inquiry. In this space, learning should be possible for both the community and the students. That is, the event should not be a one-way flow of information from students to the community; rather, students should also be able to listen and learn from the community. Implicitly, the focal place is also in conversation with both the community and the students, as it has a central role in framing the event.

Equity and Inclusion

Be mindful of who is and who is not invited to a community event. The people you invite implicitly teach your students about who is valuable in the community and who might consider their inquiry projects valuable (e.g., if you invite an all-white panel of parks staff, or use a local park as a focal place but do not invite the neighborhood community). If you are advertising the event, be intentional about the audiences that you select.

Reduce barriers for community participation in the event. Hold it at an easy-to-reach location (e.g., your school) and during dates and times that make it possible for a diverse set of people to join. If possible, improve event accessibility by providing seating, amplified sound, and interpretation using school resources. Consider also providing a remote or asynchronous participation option.

Implementation

Decide on the community you hope to engage through the event. Possible communities include:

- **Other student teams**—This is the simplest option. Student teams can present to other teams in the classroom or to other classrooms.
- **Parents/guardians**—Because working parents/guardians may not be able to visit during the school day, students can take home written materials to support family discussions and share more broadly. Consider making a booklet with printed summaries of all the students' projects or having students write illustrated letters to their families as a form of sharing. Materials should focus on showcasing students' expertise and the details of their experiences.
- **School community members**—Your school may have a community or event day on which results of inquiry projects can be shared as live performances or poster presentations; if not, consider making posters that can be displayed in an accessible place (e.g., hallway) or holding presentations during a recess or other time where other students are able to attend. To engage other students and any walk-in audience, short and lively presentations work best. To illustrate inquiry impacts to other teachers and administrators, you may want to also

include more detailed information on the structure of projects and their learning outcomes.
- **Broader community**—Brainstorm a list of people who may have a relationship with the place. Consider organizations that engage with the community (e.g., local media outlets, libraries, senior centers) or existing events that are seeking groups to share information (e.g., community health events). If hosting your own event is the only or best option, send invitations (perhaps with photos of students outside) early enough to promote participation.

If possible, hold the event in or near the location where your inquiry took place to help the community recognize and build place connections. Begin the event by recognizing connections to land (Chapter 5) and the importance of the community. The event can take a range of forms depending on your goals and the students' presentation modes. Possibilities include but are not limited to:

- Student groups sequentially present; questions from the community are answered afterward.
- Community members circulate freely among student groups, who present to each audience; questions are answered in groups.
- Student groups make presentations available asynchronously (e.g., via the Internet); community members ask questions during a later synchronous session.
- Community members share perspectives and experiences, then student groups sequentially present.
- A structured discussion among community members and student groups.

All students in each group should participate in some way in the presentation or feedback. Set expectations for students and community members that they should engage actively and respectfully with their peers when others are presenting (e.g., by being quiet while others speak and asking questions or leaving comments afterward). The event should enable bidirectional learning and reflection.

Students may be nervous about participating and presenting. Emphasize that the event should be a conversation and celebration. Make sure to recognize at least one positive thing about each team's project.

Grade-Level Differentiation

Elementary (3–5)

Sharing with parents and peers is easiest. You will need to actively structure and plan presentations for students. Students may feel shy, so offer both emotional and structural support.

Middle (6–8)

Students better understand the expectations and interests of different audiences, so you can challenge them to target their presentations accordingly. Practice and improvement with feedback are encouraged.

High (9–12)

Students can likely maintain focus for multiple practice sessions, if needed.

Examples

Figure 12.13 An evening event for family and other community members to learn about student projects

Figure 12.14 Sharing projects at a weekend community fair held at a school

Figure 12.15 A student shares her team's assessment of stream health with local officials at a town government meeting

Sharing Outcomes

Figure 12.16 Sharing project outcomes at an educational event held at a recreation area visitor center

Assessing Learning

13.1 Why (or Why Not) to Assess

Concepts

Assessing inquiry projects can sometimes be valuable. Formative assessments can help guide students' projects and build their confidence and motivation. Summative assessments can help you determine what learning has occurred and motivate engagement. Dimensions of assessment can include:

Next Generation Science Standards (NGSS):
- Content knowledge (Disciplinary Core Ideas or Crosscutting Concepts)
- Process skills (Science and Engineering Practices or otherwise)

Classroom:
- Presentation skills
- Participation

Psychosocial:
- Individual behavior
- Team behavior/interpersonal skills

Human development:

- Creativity
- Artistic sense
- Respect for and connection to place
- Community engagement

However, not all of these dimensions are easily or fairly assessed, even if they represent important axes of learning. The experience of building a relationship in a place or seeing an organism for the first time may help shift a student's long-term choices and identity in positive ways you cannot easily assess in the short term. Assessment of inquiry projects is also complicated by the open-ended nature of projects; outcomes can be unknown and surprising, and multiple pathways to excellence exist. Assess what can be measured and be humble about what cannot.

Equity and Inclusion

Grades can inadvertently reinforce power hierarchies in the classroom. Identity-related biases (e.g., around race, class, gender, beliefs, or disability) can determine how you perceive student participation and contribution, even if you think you are bias-free (Quinn, 2017; Sprietsma, 2013; Tenenbaum & Ruck, 2007). This can cause students to learn whether or not they are valued and, in turn, impact identities and future choices. Teacher-led summative assessments, especially grades, should be used cautiously in inquiry-based projects, even for apparently "objective" axes like presentation quality. Teacher-led assessment often drives motivation through fear of failure and can reduce student engagement or form a feigned, expectation-driven engagement.

Place-based inquiry projects fundamentally can and should shift power from the teacher to the students. Teacher-led assessments take some of that power away. Peer assessments come closer to supporting the power shift. Ultimately, assessment arising from students' opinions of themselves, their work, their relation to the work, or the community's opinions of the students may be most motivating and supportive of these altered power hierarchies. Deeper motivation should come from within as students seek to develop their relationships with the place.

Implementation

Decide whether you are comfortable focusing on formative assessment or also need summative assessments; if the latter, decide if you are comfortable shifting power toward student-centered approaches (implementation details in the next section). Then determine which axes of learning are most important to you, noting that some axes map most closely onto the NGSS. Focusing on a few (or no) axes for assessment can be a more effective use of your time, recognizing that additional unmeasured student growth and learning also may be occurring.

Communicate your assessment plans, and your rationale for them, before inquiry projects begin. Leave some room for feedback and revision on this process, given student input.

Grade-Level Differentiation

Elementary (3–5)

Strongly consider not assigning grades. Small and frequent formative assessments, progress checks, and student self-assessment are more valuable.

Middle (6–8)

As noted earlier.

High (9–12)

Provide more time for self-reflection. Have students assess their progress at least during and after the project.

Assessing Learning

Examples

Figure 13.1 Friendships and cultures of care develop through intensive teamwork

Figure 13.2 Time spent outside helps develop a sense of wonder and belonging

13.2 Student-Centered Reflection and Feedback

Concepts

"Ungrading" (Blum, 2020; Feldman, 2018) can shift power back to students in both formative and summative assessment. You still provide clear expectations and standards to students. However, students make progress toward these targets primarily through reflective and peer-based mechanisms, then use this process to propose their own grades. Key features include:

- Clear and transparent expectations that are communicated in advance
- Student feedback to peers within and between small groups
- Student reflection on their learning and progress in collaboration with you
- Opportunities for students to revise or improve work/behavior
- Trust that students are often capable of knowing their learning
- Focus on growth and progress
- Recognition that assessment is one of many learning tools, not a learning goal

Equity and Inclusion

Adjusting students' proposed grades is subject to the same biases as traditional grading approaches. Similarly, students of some identities may be more likely to give themselves high performance ratings. If you can avoid grades, skip them but keep the rubrics and reflection. Focus on identifying moments of growth and next steps as opposed to completion of tasks.

Implementation

Set clear expectations early on about the assessment structure and how students will participate in it. In general, rubrics and reflection should be

Assessing Learning

used together to generate final grades (if needed) through a student-led and teacher-supported conversation.

Review rubrics (examples in Appendix 3) with students in advance of projects. Students can also co-create rubrics. If you have prior student work or completed rubrics or reflections available, have your current students review these to calibrate their expectations. When using prior student work, be clear that students do not need to replicate prior project to be successful.

Rubrics can be used several times throughout a project and at least once midway through. Students should self-evaluate their projects or potentially evaluate the projects of peers. If you do peer evaluations, set expectations that critical feedback should be accompanied by positive feedback. Review feedback before sharing it to screen potentially hurtful comments. After applying the rubric, provide time for students to reflect on the rubric outcomes. Reflection questions can include:

- What areas are you succeeding in?
- Which areas are you not yet succeeding in?
- Why is this aspect of the project hard?
- What do you, your peers, or your teacher need to do differently for you to succeed?
- What should you, your peers, or your teacher keep on doing?

Revisiting team contracts and doing team check-ins (Chapter 6) effectively provide formative assessment focused on psychosocial axes.

At the end of a project, students can go through the rubric and reflection process again, using both as evidence to propose a grade (if needed). Some of this process can parallel, or occur at the same time as, overall project reflection (Chapter 11). Reflection questions can include:

- What areas did you succeed in?
- What areas did you struggle in?
- Based on your reflection and the rubrics, what grade would you recommend for yourself/your team?

Students can make their grade proposals via a written document or via a conversation with you. By allowing revision of work without penalty,

Assessing Learning

or by reducing the potential impact of a single grade on the student's overall success, this process can focus on growth-centered evaluation. You can adjust a student's grade from their proposal if needed, but doing this frequently indicates you should improve your rubric/reflection process.

In inquiry projects, providing revision opportunities can be difficult because of time or place-access constraints. Do a formative assessment early so that students have maximum time available to revise their projects.

Grade-Level Differentiation

Elementary (3–5)

Students can share "wows" (what they liked/were impressed by) and "wonders" (what else they imagine would be interesting) about their peers' projects.

Examples

Figure 13.3 Providing peer feedback on projects

Assessing Learning

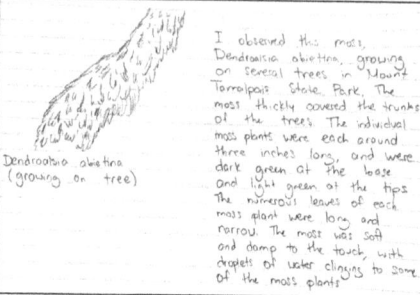

Peer feedback: The sentences are not dragging on and they are very clear to read. Very good terminology as well. The writer could have mentioned what other mosses grew in the area but they do mention that this moss covers lots of the area. Very detailed drawing as well!

Figure 13.4 Written peer feedback on an observation

Figure 13.5 Post-project journaling and reflection

Assessing Learning

Figure 13.6 Reflecting on a project at sunset

14 Conclusion

14.1 What Students and Teachers Say

Place-based scientific inquiry is an effective and accessible tool for teaching and learning outside. It can make a real difference for your students. Here are a few viewpoints from partners, primarily at Title I–eligible schools in Arizona:

> You know, this is the way science should be taught to us. The real-world experience has made science more exciting to me instead of the boring stuff we read in books. I could really get into being a scientist if I got to do this type of work every day.
>
> – Student

> [I developed] a sense of wonder... we literally had things to wonder about that we could sit in [the forest's] shade and rip the leaves off them kinda thing, that's not the same thing with having the models.... Studying models is not as cool as studying trees.
>
> – Student

> [T]he data analysis... was really cool because we're actually using it to, like, answer questions.... [But with classroom] homework, it was just answering random questions ...
>
> – Student

> What helped me a lot was the hands-on component. In school, most of the kids are fully sighted, right? Most things are watching or seeing only, where we

were out in the field doing experiments and testing things and feeling things, which helped a lot.

— Student (visually impaired)

[Doing inquiry] has been an amazing experience for me. . . [it] has already made me less anxious about leaving home for college and made me understand I can study whatever I want.

— Student

I think having the students collect data to answer a question. . . is an important thing for young scientists to know how to do. The data collection. . . engaged students. I also appreciated that the students were also given time to explore and ask questions of their own. [This can] ... offer my students so much—the opportunity to be outdoors, do field science, engage in scientific inquiry. . .

— Teacher

I love the way [this helps]. . . the kids to make observations, formulate hypotheses, and then figure out a way to collect data and evidence to support conclusions.. . . I love the way you all used the [outdoors]. . . to teach science concepts.. . . It is the perfect setting to encourage student exploration, curiosity, and discovery.

— Teacher

[These] methods are new to me, and I enjoyed seeing the students develop community, knowledge of social justice, environmental issues, and diversity.

— Teacher

[This is] a great opportunity to start and create real and lasting changes in our communities.

— Teacher

14.2 Overcoming Common Fears

If you do not know what students could study, take a walk around the school or the neighborhood, and try one of the observation/question generation activities. Every place can be interesting and valuable with open eyes.

If you do not know how much time you will need, start with a small and structured project, and follow the sample schedules. Budget at least a

Conclusion

month in advance to think through your planning. Double your initial time estimates for active instruction to accommodate the unforeseen.

If you are worried about risk and discomfort outside, start close by. Pick places that are close to indoor spaces (e.g., school playgrounds) and take frequent breaks.

If you feel that you do not know enough about the natural world, scientific equipment, or the focal place, you can learn alongside your students. Start with simpler projects and simpler tools and familiar places. You can model the process of learning alongside your students.

If you think that you cannot manage many student groups simultaneously, start with a whole-class inquiry project where multiple small groups work together on the same question. Or invest time in securing volunteers so you can reach a viable student-to-adult ratio.

If you think that your students will lose respect for you if you are no longer in charge, they instead will gain respect for you as a facilitator, as their learning becomes centered around their own interests. Student-led inquiry can help you better include students who are not readily engaged by classroom work or who frequently experience behavioral challenges.

14.3 Starting Small and Dreaming Big

Place-based scientific inquiry outside is very different from traditional classroom instruction. Making the transition is nontrivial and takes time. Give yourself the grace of starting small and dreaming big.

Small steps also build your confidence and promote your learning. You may find it takes a few trial runs to develop the necessary facilitation and group management skills and to get familiar with the flow of a project within your time constraints. Start with a relatively short project with limited scope. Your schoolyard or parking lot is a simple place to get started, and to fall back on, if you experience challenges.

Small steps and small inquiry projects will help get your students ready for larger successes later on. Once your students become familiar with open-ended inquiry and see you as the facilitator, you will find it possible to incorporate similar approaches into other projects or lessons you are already doing in the classroom. For example, labs where students are meant to get a fixed result can be replaced by ones where the students do not know the outcome or can choose their own methods.

These small steps ultimately create large changes for you and your students. You are also developing a facilitation toolkit that ultimately will let you spend less time on preparation, instruction, and student management. You are developing a group of students who are ready to learn for themselves and who are ready to see you as a partner in their learning. You are moving toward a more student-centered and justice-focused classroom. You are working to dismantle power structures that hold students back from the successes they deserve. You are building relationships and community. You are connecting people to places and working toward healing.

You are at the end of this book, and the beginning of your experience.

References

Alim, H. S., & Paris, D. (2017). What is culturally sustaining pedagogy and why does it matter. In *Culturally sustaining pedagogies: Teaching and learning for justice in a changing world*. Teachers College Press.

Anderson, M. K. (2005). *Tending the wild: Native American knowledge and the management of California's natural resources*. University of California Press.

Baglieri, S., & Lalvani, P. (2019). *Undoing ableism: Teaching about disability in K-12 classrooms*. Routledge.

Baldwin, J. (1963). A talk to teachers. *The Saturday Review, 21 December*.

Bang, M., Curley, L., Kessel, A., Marin, A., Suzukovich, E. S., & Strack, G. (2014). Muskrat theories, tobacco in the streets, and living Chicago as Indigenous land. *Environmental Education Research, 20*(1), 37–55.

Bang, M., & Medin, D. (2010). Cultural processes in science education: Supporting the navigation of multiple epistemologies. *Science Education, 94*(6), 1008–1026.

Basso, K. H. (1996). *Wisdom sits in places: Landscape and language among the Western Apache*. University of New Mexico Press.

Baurhoo, N., & Asghar, A. (2014). Using universal design for learning to construct inclusive science classrooms for diverse learners. *Learning Landscapes, 7*(2), 59–81.

Blum, S. D. (2020). *Ungrading: Why rating students undermines learning (and what to do instead)*. West Virginia University Press.

Bordessa, K. (2005). *Team challenges: 170+ group activities to build cooperation, communication, and creativity*. Zephyr Press.

Braaten, M., & Windschitl, M. (2011). Working toward a stronger conceptualization of scientific explanation for science education. *Science Education, 95*(4), 639–669.

Bratman, G. N., Hamilton, J. P., Hahn, K. S., Daily, G. C., & Gross, J. J. (2015). Nature experience reduces rumination and subgenual prefrontal cortex activation. *Proceedings of the National Academy of Sciences, 112*(28), 8567–8572.

Cajete, G. (1999). *Igniting the sparkle: An Indigenous science education model*. Kivaki Press.

Cajete, G. (2000). *Native science: Natural laws of interdependence*. Clear Light Publishers.

Chakrabarti, P. (2017). *Materials and medicine: Trade, conquest and therapeutics in the eighteenth century*. Manchester University Press.

Chen, X. (2013). STEM attrition: College students' paths into and out of STEM fields. *National Center for Education Statistics, Statistical Analysis Report 2014–001*.

Cornell, J. (2015). *Sharing nature: Nature awareness activities for all ages*. Crystal Clarity.

Cronon, W. (1996). The trouble with wilderness: Or, getting back to the wrong nature. *Environmental History, 1*(1), 7–28.

Dunbar-Ortiz, R. (2014). *An Indigenous peoples' history of the United States*. Beacon Press.

Engemann, K., Pedersen, C. B., Arge, L., Tsirogiannis, C., Mortensen, P. B., & Svenning, J.-C. (2019). Residential green space in childhood is associated with lower risk of psychiatric disorders from adolescence into adulthood. *Proceedings of the National Academy of Sciences, 116*(11), 5188–5193.

Feldman, J. (2018). *Grading for equity: What it is, why it matters, and how it can transform schools and classrooms*. Corwin Press.

Finney, C. (2014). *Black faces, white spaces: Reimagining the relationship of African Americans to the great outdoors*. University of North Carolina Press.

Fletcher, M.-S., Hamilton, R., Dressler, W., & Palmer, L. (2021). Indigenous knowledge and the shackles of wilderness. *Proceedings of the National Academy of Sciences, 118*(40), e2022218118.

Freire, P. (1970). *Pedagogy of the oppressed*. Seabury Press.

References

Frye, M. (1983). *The politics of reality: Essays in feminist theory*. Crossing Press.

Fuller, S. (2004). *Kuhn vs. Popper: The struggle for the soul of science*. Columbia University Press.

Fulton, L., & Campbell, B. (2014). *Science notebooks* (2nd ed.). Heinemann Educational Books.

Gay, G. (2018). *Culturally responsive teaching: Theory, research, and practice*. Teachers College Press.

Gibson, H. L., & Chase, C. (2002). Longitudinal impact of an inquiry-based science program on middle school students' attitudes toward science. *Science Education, 86*(5), 693–705.

Ho, Y. C. J., & Chang, D. (2021). To whom does this place belong? Whiteness and diversity in outdoor recreation and education. *Annals of Leisure Research, 25*(5), 569–582.

hooks, bell. (1994). *Teaching to transgress: Education as the practice of freedom*. Routledge.

Jack, G. (2010). Place matters: The significance of place attachments for children's well-being. *British Journal of Social Work, 40*(3), 755–771.

Jacob, M. M., Gonzales, K. L., Chappell Belcher, D., Ruef, J. L., & RunningHawk Johnson, S. (2021). Indigenous cultural values counter the damages of white settler colonialism. *Environmental Sociology, 7*(2), 134–146.

Jampel, C. (2018). Intersections of disability justice, racial justice and environmental justice. *Environmental Sociology, 4*(1), 122–135.

Johnson, V. A. (2017). Bringing together feminist disability studies and environmental justice. In *Disability studies and the environmental humanities: Toward an eco-crip theory* (pp. 201–241). University of Nebraska Press.

Jones, K., & Okun, T. (2001). White supremacy culture. In *Dismantling racism: A workbook for social change groups*. Change Work.

Kant, J., Burckhard, S., & Meyers, R. (2018). Engaging high school girls in native American culturally responsive STEAM activities. *Journal of STEM Education, 18*(5), 15–25.

Kaye, C. B. (2004). *The complete guide to service learning: Proven, practical ways to engage students in civic responsibility, academic curriculum, & social action*. Free Spirit Publishing.

Kimmerer, R. W. (2013). *Braiding sweetgrass: Indigenous wisdom, scientific knowledge and the teachings of plants*. Milkweed Editions.

Kjelvik, M. K., & Schultheis, E. H. (2019). Getting messy with authentic data: Exploring the potential of using data from scientific research to support student data literacy. *CBE—Life Sciences Education*, *18*(2), es2.

Kolonich, A., Richmond, G., & Krajcik, J. (2018). Reframing inclusive science instruction to support teachers in promoting equitable three-dimensional science classrooms. *Journal of Science Teacher Education*, *29*(8), 693–711.

Kudryavtsev, A., Stedman, R. C., & Krasny, M. E. (2012). Sense of place in environmental education. *Environmental Education Research*, *18*(2), 229–250.

Laws, J. M., & Lygren, E. (2020). *How to teach nature journaling*. Heyday Books.

Leave No Trace. (1987). *The Seven Principles of Leave No Trace*. https://lnt.org/why/7-principles/

Leonardo, Z. (2009). *Race, whiteness, and education*. Routledge.

Louv, R. (2008). *Last child in the woods: Saving our children from nature-deficit disorder*. Algonquin Books.

MacKenzie, T. (2016). *Dive into inquiry: Amplify learning and empower student voice*. EdTechTeam Press.

MacKerron, G., & Mourato, S. (2013). Happiness is greater in natural environments. *Global Environmental Change*, *23*(5), 992–1000.

Maguvhe, M. (2015). Teaching science and mathematics to students with visual impairments: Reflections of a visually impaired technician. *African Journal of Disability*, *4*(1), 1–6.

Marlowe, B. A., & Page, M. L. (2005). *Creating and sustaining the constructivist classroom*. Corwin Press.

Marshall, J. C., & Alston, D. M. (2014). Effective, sustained inquiry-based instruction promotes higher science proficiency among all groups: A 5-year analysis. *Journal of Science Teacher Education*, *25*(7), 807–821.

McCarty, T., & Lee, T. (2014). Critical culturally sustaining/revitalizing pedagogy and Indigenous education sovereignty. *Harvard Educational Review*, *84*(1), 101–124.

References

Minner, D. D., Levy, A. J., & Century, J. (2010). Inquiry-based science instruction—What is it and does it matter? Results from a research synthesis years 1984 to 2002. *Journal of Research in Science Teaching, 47*(4), 474–496.

Moon, N. W., Todd, R. L., Morton, D. L., & Ivey, E. (2012). *Accommodating students with disabilities in science, technology, engineering, and mathematics (STEM)*. Center for Assistive Technology and Environmental Access College of Architecture, Georgia Institute of Technology. https://hourofcode.com/files/accommodating-students-with-disabilities.pdf

Murawksi, W., & Scott, K. L. (2019). *What really works with universal design for learning*. Corwin Press.

National Research Council. (2012). *A framework for K-12 science education: Practices, crosscutting concepts, and core ideas*. National Academies Press.

Nxumalo, F. (2019). *Decolonizing place in early childhood education*. Routledge.

Odeny, B., & Bosurgi, R. (2022). Time to end parachute science. *PLoS Medicine, 19*(9), e1004099.

Oyler, C. (2012). *Actions speak louder than words: Community activism as curriculum*. Routledge.

Pfund, C., House, S., Asquith, P., Spencer, K., Silet, K., & Sorkness, C. (2012). *Mentor training for clinical and translational researchers*. W. H. Freeman.

Platt, J. R. (1964). Strong inference: Certain systematic methods of scientific thinking may produce much more rapid progress than others. *Science, 146*(3642), 347–353.

Price, K., Eller, R., & Murr, J. (2015). *Team building activities for STEM groups: 50 fun activities to keep STEM learners engaged!* Paradigm Shift.

Quinn, D. M. (2017). Racial attitudes of PreK–12 and postsecondary educators: Descriptive evidence from nationally representative data. *Educational Researcher, 46*(7), 397–411.

Relph, E. (1976). *Place and placelessness*. Pion.

Riggs, E. M. (2005). Field-based education and Indigenous knowledge: Essential components of geoscience education for native American communities. *Science Education, 89*(2), 296–313.

Rivera Maulucci, M. S., Brown, B. A., Grey, S. T., & Sullivan, S. (2014). Urban middle school students' reflections on authentic science inquiry. *Journal of Research in Science Teaching, 51*(9), 1119–1149.

Roy, R. D. (2018). Science still bears the fingerprints of colonialism. *Smithsonian Magazine*.

RunningHawk Johnson, S. (2018). Native philosophy as the basis for secondary science curriculum. *Critical Education, 9*(16), 84–97.

Ryan, R. M., Weinstein, N., Bernstein, J., Brown, K. W., Mistretta, L., & Gagne, M. (2010). Vitalizing effects of being outdoors and in nature. *Journal of Environmental Psychology, 30*(2), 159–168.

Scheiner, S., & Gurevitch, J. (Eds.). (2019). *Design and analysis of ecological experiments*. CRC Press.

Schwarz, C. V., Passmore, C., & Reiser, B. J. (2017). *Helping students make sense of the world using next generation science and engineering practices*. NSTA Press.

Semken, S., & Freeman, C. B. (2008). Sense of place in the practice and assessment of place-based science teaching. *Science Education, 92*(6), 1042–1057.

Smith, L. T. (1999). *Decolonizing methodologies: Research and Indigenous peoples*. Bloomsbury Publishing.

Snively, G., & Corsiglia, J. (2001). Discovering Indigenous science: Implications for science education. *Science Education, 85*(1), 6–34.

Sobel, D. (2004). *Place-based education: Connecting classroom and community*. Orion Society.

Sprietsma, M. (2013). Discrimination in grading: Experimental evidence from primary school teachers. *Empirical Economics, 45*(1), 523–538.

Stevenson, R. B. (2008). A critical pedagogy of place and the critical place(s) of pedagogy. *Environmental Education Research, 14*(3), 353–360.

Taylor, D. E. (2016). *The rise of the American conservation movement: Power, privilege, and environmental protection*. Duke University Press.

Taylor, S. (2021). Age of disability: On living well with impaired landscapes. *Orion Magazine, (winter)*.

Tenenbaum, H. R., & Ruck, M. D. (2007). Are teachers' expectations different for racial minority than for European American students? A meta-analysis. *Journal of Educational Psychology, 99*, 253–273.

References

Tuck, E., McKenzie, M., & McCoy, K. (2014). Land education: Indigenous, post-colonial, and decolonizing perspectives on place and environmental education research. *Environmental Education Research, 20*(1), 1–23.

Tuck, E., & Yang, K. W. (2012). Decolonization is not a metaphor. *Decolonization Indignity, Education & Society, 1*(1), 1–40.

Tuckman, B. W. (1965). Developmental sequence in small groups. *Psychological Bulletin, 63*(6), 384.

Valle, G. R. (2021). Narratives of place: Critical reflections on place-making in the curriculum of environmental studies and sciences (ESS). *Journal of Environmental Studies and Sciences, 11*(1), 130–138.

Van Ness, D., & Strong, K. H. (2014). *Restoring justice: An introduction to restorative justice*. Routledge.

Wilson, S. (2008). *Research is ceremony: Indigenous research methods*. Fernwood Publishing.

Windschitl, M., Thompson, J., & Braaten, M. (2018). *Ambitious science teaching*. Harvard Educational Publishing Group.

Zelenski, J. M., Dopko, R. L., & Capaldi, C. A. (2015). Cooperation is in our nature: Nature exposure may promote cooperative and environmentally sustainable behavior. *Journal of Environmental Psychology, 42*, 24–31.

Zinn, H. (2015). *A people's history of the United States: 1492-present*. Routledge.

Zoldosova, K., & Prokop, P. (2006). Education in the field influences children's ideas and interest toward science. *Journal of Science Education and Technology, 15*(3), 304–313.

Index

Notes: *Italicised* page numbers refer to figures and **bold** refers to tables in the text.

accessibility 38, 68
access to additional supplies 66
acknowledging 133; different skills 105; resolving conflicts and 119
additional supplies, access to 66
alienated 111
allowing all voices to be heard 104–105
allowing students to discuss in pairs 100
American Sign Language (ASL) 50, *52*, 56
analysis of variance (ANOVA) 213, *216*
analyzing and sense-making 198–217; drawing conclusions from data 198–204; statistical tests 212–217; visually interpreting results 205–211
anchor chart 138; blank 157; class whiteboard 158; generic *157*; hypotheses component of 156; with study design predetermined by the teacher *159*; verbal or graphical predictions on 199; *see also* designing a study and using an anchor chart
animals: behavior 201; noises 121; place use 80; questions 146

answering questions with more questions 100
artists/illustrator 180, *182*
asking general questions 100
asking probing questions 100
asking process questions 100
asking questions that do not have yes/no answers 100
asking specific time-centered questions 100
assessing learning 243–251; student-centered reflection and feedback 247–251; why (or why not) to assess 243–246
auditory equipment 81; *see also* equipment and data collection at low cost
avoiding stereotypes 43

background information, acquiring 87–90; concepts 87; elementary (3–5) 88; equity and inclusion 87; examples 88, *89*, 90; grade-level differentiation 88; high (9–12) 88; implementation 87–88; middle (6–8) 88
bad handwriting 187

263

Index

barriers minimizing 43
basic needs 66
being comfortable with some chaos 130
blindfolded: search 121; student 82, 84, 187
blind/low vision students 50–51; accessibility 38, 54, 65, 68, 238; colorblind 205; technology 9, 13, 51, 178
boundaries 67
broader community 239
building a strong question 141–147; concepts 141–142, **142–143**; elementary (3–5) 145; equity and inclusion 144; examples 146, *147*; grade-level differentiation 145–146; high (9–12) 146; implementation 144–145; middle (6–8) 146

centering student identity 10–12
chaos, being comfortable 130
check-ins, having regular 130
circle observations 82
classroom 243
close observation activity 138
close observation drawing 80
codes 187
collecting data 185–192; concepts 185–186; elementary (3–5) 188; examples *188–192*; grade-level differentiation 188; implementation 186–188
collecting data outdoors 183–197; collecting data 185–192; practicing collecting data 183–185; securing data 192–197
colonization 15–16
color rainbow 82
communicating expectations 66
communicating schedules 66

communication skills, building of 121–122
communication tools 67
community event 237–242; concepts 237; elementary (3–5) 240; equity and inclusion 238; examples *240–242*; grade-level differentiation 240; high (9–12) 240; implementation 238–239; middle (6–8) 240
concepts: acquiring background information 87; acquiring equipment and collecting data at low cost 58; building a strong question 141–142, **142–143**; choosing a topic 24; choosing how much to measure 172–173; choosing roles 179; choosing what to do (protocols, checklists, and datasheets) 176; collecting data 185–186; cost considerations 35; designing a study and using an anchor chart 147–156 *148*; dividing students into groups 73; drawing conclusions from data 198–200; encouraging positive behavior from groups 113–114; encouraging positive behavior from individuals 107; exploration, observation, and sense of place 79; facilitating question development 136; getting groups back on track 132; handling multiple groups 129; holding a community event 237; how and why to share projects 226; identifying multiple hypotheses and predictions, or not 162–165; partnering with volunteers 53; place considerations 38; practicing collecting data 183; recognition 223; recognizing relationships and responsibility to place 90; reflection 218–219; role as teacher 20;

safety and logistical preparation 65; scaffolding projects into curriculum 32; scheduling and time considerations 26–27; securing data 192; setting behavioral expectations 102–103; small-group facilitation 97; statistical tests **212–213**, 212–214; student-centered reflection and feedback 247; student identity considerations 42; supporting presentation development 232; team building 118–119; team contracts and check-ins 125; universal design, special needs, and disability 46; using notebooks 75; visually interpreting results 205; why (or why not) to assess 243–244
consciousness critical 3–5, 7, 9, 19, 42
constructivism, place-based teaching 8
content linkages 38
contrasts 38
conversation on group dynamics 133
cost considerations 35–37; categories 35; concepts 35; elementary (3–5) 36; equity and inclusion 35; examples *37*; grade-level differentiation 36; high (9–12) 36; implementation 36; middle (6–8) 36
Crosscutting Concepts 218; scaffolding projects into curriculum 32, 33; scheduling and time considerations 30
culture/cultural/culturally 12, 232; artifacts 40; differences 43; erasure of 15; expectations 132; friendships and *246*; identities 12; Indigenous science 18; informed 44; meaningful places *41*; of mutual respect 27; responsive 17; supportive 43; sustaining 17; trespassing on significant sites 40; values 7, 12; *see also* white supremacy

cups/envelopes/sealable plastic bags 59
curiosity and exploration 103
curriculum *see* scaffolding projects into curriculum

data collection *see* collecting data outdoors; planning data collection
data recorder 180, *181*
data recording techniques 187
day-in-the-life 82
decolonization: discomfort 17; place-based outdoor teaching 17; place relationships and 219; teaching 15–17, 18
designing a study and using an anchor chart 147–162; concepts 147–156 *148*; elementary (3–5) 158; examples *159–160*, 161–162; grade-level differentiation 158; high (9–12) 158; implementation 156–158, *157*; middle (6–8) 158
destroying things 110
differences from home 82
digital team contract *128*
disability 22; additional support for 46; identity-related biases 50; in outdoor activities 17; student identities 21, 46; students with physical 50; *see also* universal design, special needs, and disability
Disciplinary Core Ideas, NGSS 13, 14, 26, 218; scaffolding projects into curriculum 32, 33; scheduling and time considerations 30
discrimination, marginalization and 11
disengaging from the group 109
distance 38

265

Index

dividing students into groups 73–75; concepts 73; elementary (3–5) 74; equity and inclusion 73; examples 75; grade-level differentiation 74; high (9–12) 74; implementation 74; middle (6–8) 74

doing nothing 133

dominating/directing others 109

drawing conclusions from data 198–204; concepts 198–200; elementary (3–5) 201–202; equity and inclusion 200; examples 202–204; grade-level differentiation 201–202; high (9–12) 202; implementation 201; middle (6–8) 202

dreaming big 254–255

durability 38

education, empowering young people 4

elementary school (3–5): acquiring background information 88; building a strong question 145; choosing a topic 25; choosing how much to measure 174; choosing what to do (protocols, checklists, and datasheets) 178; collecting data 188; cost considerations 36; designing a study and using an anchor chart 158; dividing students into groups 74; drawing conclusions from data 201–202; encouraging positive behavior from groups 116; facilitating question development 138; getting groups back on track 134; handling multiple groups 130; holding a community event 240; how and why to share projects 228; identifying multiple hypotheses and predictions, or not 169; partnering with volunteers 55; place considerations 40; practicing collecting data 184; recognition 224; reflection 221; role as teacher 22; safety and logistical preparation 69; scaffolding projects into curriculum 33; scheduling and time considerations 29; securing data 194; setting behavioral expectations 105; statistical tests 214–215; student-centered reflection and feedback 249; student identity considerations 43–44; supporting presentation development 234; team building 123; team contracts and check-ins 127; using notebooks 76; visually interpreting results 207; why (or why not) to assess 245

English language learners 50

equipment 68; auditory 81; keeper 180; misuse 187; tactile 81–82; visual 80–81; writing 82

equipment and data collection at: concepts 58; equity and inclusion 59; examples 61–64; grade-level differentiation 60; high (9–12) 60; implementation 59–60; low cost 58–64

equity and inclusion: acquiring background information 87; acquiring equipment and collecting data at low cost 59; building a strong question 144; choosing a topic 24; choosing roles 180; choosing what to do (protocols, checklists, and datasheets) 177; cost considerations 35; dividing students into groups 73; drawing conclusions from data 200; encouraging positive behavior from groups 114; encouraging positive behavior from individuals 107; exploration, observation,

266

and sense of place 79; facilitating question development 136–137; getting groups back on track 132; handling multiple groups 129; holding a community event 238; how and why to share projects 227; identifying multiple hypotheses and predictions, or not 165; partnering with volunteers 53–54; place considerations 39; practicing collecting data 183; recognition 223; recognizing relationships and responsibility to place 90–91; reflection 219; role as teacher 20; safety and logistical preparation 65–66; scheduling and time considerations 27; setting behavioral expectations 103; small-group facilitation 97–98; statistical tests 214; student-centered reflection and feedback 247; student identity considerations 42; supporting presentation development 232; team building 119; team contracts and check-ins 126; universal design, special needs, and disability 46–47; using notebooks 76; visually interpreting results 205–206; why (or why not) to assess 244–245

ethics 38; building a strong question 141; co-discovery journey with students 91; hypothesis-testing study design 148; protocol 177; respect and 92; information 88, 89, 90; acquiring equipment and collecting data at low cost 61–64; building a strong question 146, 147; choosing a topic 26; choosing how much to measure 175–176; choosing roles 181–182; choosing what to do (protocols, checklists, and datasheets) 179; collecting data 188–192; cost considerations 37; designing a study and using an anchor chart 159–160, 161–162; dividing students into groups 75; drawing conclusions from data 202–204; encouraging positive behavior from groups 117–118; encouraging positive behavior from individuals 112–113; exploration, observation, and sense of place 83–86; facilitating question development 139, 140–141; getting groups back on track 135; handling multiple groups 131; holding a community event 240–242; how and why to share projects 229–231; identifying multiple hypotheses and predictions, or not 170–172; partnering with volunteers 56–58; place considerations 40–41; practicing collecting data 184–185; recognition 225; recognizing relationships and responsibility to place 93–94, 94–95, 95–96; reflection 222; role as teacher 22; safety and logistical preparation 69–72; scaffolding projects into curriculum 34; scheduling and time considerations 30, 30–31; securing data 194–197; setting behavioral expectations 106–107; small-group facilitation 101–102; statistical tests 215, 216–217; student-centered reflection and feedback 249–251; student identity considerations 44–45; supporting presentation development 234–237; team building 123–125; team contracts and check-ins 127–128; universal design, special needs, and disability 51–52; using notebooks 77–78; visually interpreting results 207–211, 208–210; why (or why not) to assess 246

Index

expectations *see* scope and expectations
exploration, observation, and sense of place 79–86; concepts 79; equity and inclusion 79; examples *83–86*; implementation 79–83
exploration and team building 73–96; acquiring background information 87–90; dividing students into groups 73–75; exploration, observation, and sense of place 79–86; recognizing relationships and responsibility to place 90–96; using notebooks 75–78
explorer 180
exploring the environment 108
expressing prejudices 110
extra supplies 68

facilitative question-based approach 98
facilities 67
factual correctness 100
feasible protocol 177
feeling afraid 110
feeling alienated 111
feeling uncomfortable 111
504 plan 48–49
five senses observations 137
five things in common 120
float between groups 129–130
forecasting 111
forest/lake area, question 139
free write 82
Freire, P. 3
Frye, M. 10

gender: identity-related biases 244; student being powerful or oppressed 10; student identity 4, 21
getting groups back on track 132–135; concepts 132; elementary (3–5) 134; equity and inclusion 132; examples *135*; grade-level differentiation 134; implementation 133–134
getting to know names and each other 120–121
grade-level differentiation: acquiring background information 88; acquiring equipment and collecting data at low cost 60; building a strong question 145–146; choosing a topic 25; choosing how much to measure 174; choosing what to do (protocols, checklists, and datasheets) 178; collecting data 188; cost considerations 36; designing a study and using an anchor chart 158; dividing students into groups 74; drawing conclusions from data 201–202; encouraging positive behavior from groups 116; facilitating question development 138–139; getting groups back on track 134; handling multiple groups 130; holding a community event 240; how and why to share projects 228; identifying multiple hypotheses and predictions, or not 169; partnering with volunteers 55; place considerations 40; practicing collecting data 184; recognition 224–225; recognizing relationships and responsibility to place 92; reflection 221–222; role as teacher 22; safety and logistical preparation 69; scaffolding projects into curriculum 33; scheduling and time considerations 29–30; securing data 194; setting behavioral expectations 105; statistical tests 214–215; student-centered reflection and feedback 249; student identity considerations 43–44; supporting

presentation development 234; team building 123; team contracts and check-ins 127; using notebooks 76; visually interpreting results 207; why (or why not) to assess 245

group dynamics 27; conversation on 133; help the group 98; invest in team building 43; parents/guardians complicating 54; plan for flexibility 28; positive 112; self-regulation in 116; student engagement and 97; students self-awareness of 98; team building 115

guided poem 82

guidelines, establishing and communicating 43

helping the group 108

high school (9–12): acquiring background information 88; acquiring equipment and collecting data at low cost 60; building a strong question 146; choosing a topic 25; choosing how much to measure 174; cost considerations 36; designing a study and using an anchor chart 158; dividing students into groups 74; drawing conclusions from data 202; encouraging positive behavior from groups 116; facilitating question development 139; handling multiple groups 130; holding a community event 240; how and why to share projects 228; identifying multiple hypotheses and predictions, or not 169; place considerations 40; recognition 225; reflection 222; role as teacher 22; safety and logistical preparation 69; scaffolding projects into curriculum 33; scheduling and time considerations 30; statistical tests 215; student identity considerations 44; team contracts and check-ins 127; visually interpreting results 207; why (or why not) to assess 245

how and why to share projects 226–231; concepts 226; elementary (3–5) 228; equity and inclusion 227; examples *229–231*; grade-level differentiation 228; high (9–12) 228; implementation 227–228; middle (6–8) 228

human development 244

human knot 121

human place use 80

hypotheses 162–164; *see also* identifying multiple hypotheses and predictions, or not

hypothesis-driven projects 199, 205

hypothesis-testing study design 148

"I am like" poem 82

ice cube trays 59

identifying multiple hypotheses and predictions, or not 162–172; concepts 162–165; elementary (3–5) 169; equity and inclusion 165; examples *170–172*; grade-level differentiation 169; high (9–12) 169; implementation 165–168; middle (6–8) 169

identity *see* student identity

identity-based marginalization 11

implementation: acquiring background information 87–88; acquiring equipment and collecting data at low cost 59–60; building a strong question 144–145; choosing a topic 24–25; choosing how much to measure 173–174; choosing roles 180; choosing what to do (protocols, checklists, and datasheets) 177–178; collecting data 186–188; cost considerations 36; designing a study and using an anchor chart 156–158, *157*; dividing students into groups 74; drawing conclusions from data 201; encouraging positive behavior from groups 115–116; encouraging positive behavior from individuals 107–112; exploration, observation, and sense of place 79–83; facilitating question development 137–138; getting groups back on track 133–134; handling multiple groups 129–130; holding a community event 238–239; how and why to share projects 227–228; identifying multiple hypotheses and predictions, or not 165–168; partnering with volunteers 54–55; place considerations 39–40; practicing collecting data 183–184; recognition 223–224; recognizing relationships and responsibility to place 91–92; reflection 219–221; role as teacher 21–22; safety and logistical preparation 66–68; scaffolding projects into curriculum 33; scheduling and time considerations 27–29; securing data 192–193; setting behavioral expectations 103–105; small-group facilitation 98–100; statistical tests 214; student-centered reflection and feedback 247–249; student identity considerations 42–43; supporting presentation development 232–233; team building 119–122; team contracts and check-ins 126; universal design, special needs, and disability 47–51; using notebooks 76; visually interpreting results 206; why (or why not) to assess 245

improving behavior 108

inclusive protocol 177

Indigenous: name 91; peoples 1, 15, 17, 90, 92; perspectives 19; rights 38, 90, 92; science 18–19; students 7, 18, 19, 90, *93*; wilderness 17

Individualized Education Plan 27, 48–49

information 66–67; representation 47

inquiry-based teaching 7–8, 11; benefits of 8; perspective 18

interviews 81

introducing partner (paired activity) 120

Jones, K. 11

justice-first science teaching 3–4, 10

kitchen/luggage scale 59
kitchen thermometers 59
kitchen timers 59

land acknowledgment 92
land education, place-based inquiry linked to 8
laser eyes 122
lava lake 122
lava river 121–122, *124*
Leave No Trace principles 67, 104
Leonardo, Z. 11
level 59
Leveraging Crosscutting Concepts, NGSS 13–14
linear regression 213–215, *216*
logistics 38
lost equipment 186; *see also* equipment; equipment and data collection at low cost
lost notebooks/pencils 187

magic stick 121, *123*
magnifying lens/tweezers 59
marginalization: discrimination and 11; identity-based 11; role of teaching outdoors in combatting 11; within student groups 98
measure, choosing how to 172–176; concepts 172–173; elementary (3–5) 174; examples *175–176*; grade-level differentiation 174; high (9–12) 174; implementation 173–174; middle (6–8) 174
measuring tape/meter stick 59
medical: equipment 35; forms for information 66; situations 67; training 54; *see also* partnering with volunteers; safety and logistical preparation
meditative/reflective 83
meet a tree 82, *84*
mental breaks 119
mental map 83
mental picture 166
middle school (6–8): acquiring background information 88; building a strong question 146; choosing a topic 25; choosing how much to measure 174; choosing what to do (protocols, checklists, and datasheets) 178; designing a study and using an anchor chart 158; dividing students into groups 74; drawing conclusions from data 202; encouraging positive behavior from groups 116; facilitating question development 138–139; handling multiple groups 130; holding a community event 240; how and why to share projects 228; identifying multiple hypotheses and predictions, or not 169; place considerations 40; recognition 224; recognizing relationships and responsibility to place 92; reflection 222; role as teacher 22; safety and logistical preparation 69; scaffolding projects into curriculum 33; scheduling and time considerations 30; securing data 194; setting behavioral expectations 105; statistical tests 215; student identity considerations 44; supporting presentation development 234; team building 123; team contracts and check-ins 127; visually interpreting results 207
monster game 122, *125*
morphonames 187, *192*
motivation of students 4
multiple groups, handling 129–131; concepts 129; elementary (3–5) 130; equity and inclusion 129; examples 131; grade-level differentiation 130; high (9–12) 130; implementation 129–130; middle (6–8) 130
multiple hypotheses 142, 163, 199; *see also* identifying multiple hypotheses and predictions, or not

names, getting to know 120–121
natural art 81
natural history notes 81
neurodiverse students 49–50
Next Generation Science Standards (NGSS) 12–14, 243; learning as three-dimensional 13; learning beyond 14–15; student-led inquiry 32
Nez Perce *41*, *93*
normalizing having needs 66
norms 102

Index

notebooks, use of 75–78; concepts 75; elementary (3–5) 76; equity and inclusion 76; examples 77–78; grade-level differentiation 76; implementation 76

observations, making 108
Okun, T. 11
open-ended questions 100; see also question and study design, developing of
outcomes see sharing outcomes
oven 59
overcoming common fears 253–254
oversharing opinions/facts 109

packing lists 68
paint sample booklet 59
paired drawing 81
paper damage 187
parents/guardians 239; care taken when recruiting 53; making group dynamics complicate 54; not to be solicited for funding student needs 59; time spent by community volunteer organizations in lieu of 53–54
partnering with volunteers 53–58; concepts 53; elementary (3–5) 55; equity and inclusion 53–54; examples 56–58; grade-level differentiation 55; implementation 54–55
Pascua Yaqui 1, 44
people, questions 146
permits 38
place-based inquiry 8, 12, 13, 20, 21, 32
place-based outdoor projects 244
place-based outdoor teaching: decolonization 17; role in students' awareness 17

place-based projects 24, 227
place-based scientific inquiry 8, 252; decolonizing knowledge 16; help to removes barriers and norms common to classrooms 11; see also Next Generation Science Standards (NGSS)
place-based teaching 4–7, 10; as foundation for integrating justice for disabled students 11; perspective of knowledge 18
place considerations 38–41; concepts 38; elementary (3–5) 40; equity and inclusion 39; examples 40–41; grade-level differentiation 40; high (9–12) 40; implementation 39–40; middle (6–8) 40
place knowledge 43
placelessness, feelings of 6
planning data collection 172–182; choosing how much to measure 172–176; choosing roles 179–182; choosing what to do (protocols, checklists, and datasheets) 176–179
plants, questions 146
plastic vials 59
positive behavior from groups, encouraging 113–118; concepts 113–114; elementary (3–5) 116; equity and inclusion 114; examples 117–118; grade-level differentiation 116; high (9–12) 116; implementation 115–116; middle (6–8) 116
positive behavior from individuals, encouraging 107–113; concepts 107; equity and inclusion 107; examples 112–113; implementation 107–112
positive relationships, building 122

potentially marginalized students 49
practicing collecting data 183–185; concepts 183; elementary (3–5) 184; equity and inclusion 183; examples *184–185*; grade-level differentiation 184; implementation 183–184
praising 112
predator-prey 122, *124*
prejudices 110
pristineness/pristine 6, 11, 39, 90; *see also* wilderness/wild
proximity 111
psychosocial 243
public 67–68
PVC piping 59

quadrat 187
question and study design, developing of 136–172; building a strong question 141–147; designing a study and using an anchor chart 147–162; facilitating question development 136–141; identifying multiple hypotheses and predictions, or not 162–172
question development, facilitating 136–141; concepts 136; elementary (3–5) 138; equity and inclusion 136–137; examples 139, *140–141*; grade-level differentiation 138–139; high (9–12) 139; implementation 137–138; middle (6–8) 138–139
question generation 137–138
question templates 138
question types **142–143**

race: identity-related biases 244; student being powerful or oppressed 10; student identity 4, 21
randomization 187
recognition 223–225; concepts 223; elementary (3–5) 224; equity and inclusion 223; examples *225*; grade-level differentiation 224–225; high (9–12) 225; implementation 223–224; middle (6–8) 224
redirecting attention 111
reflecting and recognizing success 218–225; recognition 223–225; reflection 218–222
reflection 218–222; around findings 220; around justice 221; around place relationships 221; around process 220; around self/peers 220; concepts 218–219; elementary (3–5) 221; equity and inclusion 219; examples *222*; grade-level differentiation 221–222; high (9–12) 222; implementation 219–221; middle (6–8) 222
relationships 5, 83
relationships and responsibility to place 90–96; concepts 90; equity and inclusion 90–91; examples *93–94*, *94–95*, *95–96*; grade-level differentiation 92; implementation 91–92; middle (6–8) 92
Relph, E. 5
relying on other adults 130
removal/removing students 112
resonance and meaning 38
resources and planning safe logistics 53–72; acquiring equipment and collecting data at low cost 58–64; partnering with volunteers 53–58; safety and logistical preparation 65–72
respect for organisms 104
respect for others 104–105
respect for place 104

273

role as teacher 20–23; concepts 20; elementary (3–5) 22; equity and inclusion 20; examples 22; grade-level differentiation 22; high (9–12) 22; implementation 21–22; middle (6–8) 22
roles selection 179–182; concepts 179; equity and inclusion 180; examples *181–182*; implementation 180
rope shape-making 121
rubric 233, 248
rules 102

safety and logistical preparation 38, 65–72; concepts 65; elementary (3–5) 69; equity and inclusion 65–66; examples *69–72*; grade-level differentiation 69; high (9–12) 69; implementation 66–68; middle (6–8) 69
sampling techniques 187–188
scaffolding projects into curriculum 32–34; concepts 32; elementary (3–5) 33; examples *34*; grade-level differentiation 33; high (9–12) 33; implementation 33; middle (6–8) 33
scheduling and time considerations: concepts 26–27; elementary (3–5) 29; equity and inclusion 27; examples 30, *30–31*; grade-level differentiation 29–30; high (9–12) 30; implementation 27–29; middle (6–8) 30
school community members 238–239
schoolyard trash production, studying *12*
Science and Engineering Practices 13, 218; scaffolding projects into curriculum 32; scheduling and time considerations 30
scope and expectations 20–52; choosing a topic 24–31; cost considerations 35–37; place considerations 38–41; role as teacher 20–23; scaffolding projects into curriculum 32–34; student identity considerations 42–45; universal design, special needs, and disability 46–52
securing data 192–197; concepts 192; elementary (3–5) 194; examples *194–197*; grade-level differentiation 194; implementation 192–193; middle (6–8) 194
sense-making *see* analyzing and sense-making
sense of place 28, 48, 79–86; *see also* exploration, observation, and sense of place
setting behavioral expectations 102–107; concepts 102–103; elementary (3–5) 105; equity and inclusion 103; examples *106–107*; grade-level differentiation 105; implementation 103–105; middle (6–8) 105
sharing and reviewing 133
sharing outcomes 226–242; holding a community event 237–242; how and why to share projects 226–231; supporting presentation development 232–237
show and tell 138
signaling 112
silence 83
simplifying 133
small-group facilitation 97–102; concepts 97; equity and inclusion 97–98; examples *101–102*; implementation 98–100
soliciting multiple answers 100
solving problems 108
sound inventory 81
sound map 81
starting small 254–255

Index

statistical tests 212–217; concepts **212–213**, 212–214; elementary (3–5) 214–215; equity and inclusion 214; examples 215, *216–217*; grade-level differentiation 214–215; high (9–12) 215; implementation 214; middle (6–8) 215

statistics 33; descriptive 198, 205, 214; inferential 200, 212; summary 207

stereotypes 43, 54, 79, 98

string/rope 59

strong inference 163, 164, 199, 232

student(s): action and expression 47–48; behaviors 108–111; with disabilities 50; engagement 48; learning 5; motivation of 4; teams 238; view 252–253

student-centered reflection and feedback 247–251; concepts 247; elementary (3–5) 249; equity and inclusion 247; examples *249–251*; grade-level differentiation 249; implementation 247–249

student-centered teaching 10, 97

student identity *10*, 10–12, 42–45; concepts 42; elementary (3–5) 43–44; equity and inclusion 42; examples *44–45*; grade-level differentiation 43–44; high (9–12) 44; implementation 42–43; middle (6–8) 44

study design 14, 30; anchor chart with *159*; creative 15; cross-sectional 215; *see also* question and study design, developing of

suburban schoolyard, question 139

summarizing 133

supporting presentation development 232–237; concepts 232; elementary (3–5) 234; equity and inclusion 232; examples *234–237*; grade-level differentiation 234; implementation 232–233; middle (6–8) 234

tactile equipment 81–82
tactile exploration 81
taking a break 133, *135*
taking care of one another's needs 105
taking immediate action 133
task-setting 111
teachers view 252–253
teaching outside 8–10, *9*; combat marginalization of disabled students 11; schoolyard or remote sites 65
team building 43, 118–125; concepts 118–119; elementary (3–5) 123; equity and inclusion 119; examples *123–125*; grade-level differentiation 123; implementation 119–122; middle (6–8) 123; *see also* exploration and team building
team contracts and check-ins 125–128; concepts 125; elementary (3–5) 127; equity and inclusion 126; examples *127–128*; grade-level differentiation 127; high (9–12) 127; implementation 126; middle (6–8) 127
teams and conflict resolving 97–135; encouraging positive behavior from groups 113–118; encouraging positive behavior from individuals 107–113; getting groups back on track 132–135; handling multiple groups 129–131; setting behavioral expectations 102–107; small-group facilitation 97–102; team building 118–125; team contracts and check-ins 125–128
ten minutes of silence activity 137
tick marks 187

Index

time and schedule 105
timer 180
timetable for day's work 130
timing activity chunks 111
Tohono O'odham 1
tools 138, 254; communication 67; scarcity 58; for speaking and listening 115; statistical tests 200; usage 108
topic selection 24–31; concepts 24; elementary (3–5) 25; equity and inclusion 24; examples 26; grade-level differentiation 25; high (9–12) 25; implementation 24–25; middle (6–8) 25
transect 187, *191*
transportation mode 68
trowels 59
trust fall and pass-around 122
t-test 213–214, 215, *216–217*
twenty questions activity 137

ungrading 247
universal design, special needs, and disability 46–52; concepts 46; equity and inclusion 46–47; examples *51–52*; implementation 47–51; *see also* disability
Universal Design for Learning (UDL) 46
urban schoolyard, question 139

values 5, 7, 9, 12, 16, 42, 125, 136, 205, 237
valuing student suggestions 100
visual equipment 80–81
visually interpreting results 205–211; concepts 205; elementary (3–5) 207; equity and inclusion 205–206; examples *207–211*, 208–210; grade-level differentiation 207; high (9–12) 207; implementation 206; middle (6–8) 207
volunteers *see* partnering with volunteers

wait times 55, 100
wander 109–110
weather 68; animal behavior and 201; communicating expectations 66; effects of 14; inclement 76; learning to use digital meter *179*; study of natural world *31*
welfare checker 180
what to do (protocols, checklists, and datasheets) 176–179; concepts 176; elementary (3–5) 178; equity and inclusion 177; examples *179*; grade-level differentiation 178; implementation 177–178; middle (6–8) 178
white supremacy culture: discouraging conflict in favor of absolute viewpoint 114; inquiry-based teaching 11
why (or why not) to assess 243–246; concepts 243–244; elementary (3–5) 245; equity and inclusion 244–245; examples *246*; grade-level differentiation 245; high (9–12) 245; implementation 245
wilderness/wild 6, 17, 30; *see also* pristineness/pristine
withdrawing 110
writing 82; assignments 32; blog post for Internet distribution 231; drawing skills and 234; implementing a risk management plan and 65; natural history notes *85*; short observations 138

young people, education empowering *4*

For Product Safety Concerns and Information please contact our EU
representative GPSR@taylorandfrancis.com
Taylor & Francis Verlag GmbH, Kaufingerstraße 24, 80331 München, Germany

www.ingramcontent.com/pod-product-compliance
Lightning Source LLC
Chambersburg PA
CBHW052215300426
44115CB00011B/1689